THE CRITICAL MEANING
OF THE BIBLE

DEDICATION

In his address to the assembly of Bishops in Chicago, April 29, 1980, Archbishop John R. Quinn, President of the National Conference of Catholic Bishops, criticized "the intemperate attack by self-appointed guardians of orthodoxy on respected, dedicated Catholic scholars." He reminded the Bishops of the words of Pope John Paul II at the Catholic University in Washington, D.C. on October 6, 1979:

> I want to say a special word of gratitude, encouragement, and guidance for the theologians, The Church needs her theologians, particularly in this time and age so profoundly marked by deep changes in all areas of life and society. . . .We [the Bishops of the Church] all need your work, your dedication and the fruits of your reflection. We desire to listen to you, and we are eager to receive the valued assistance of your responsible scholarship.

I dedicate this book in gratitude to Archbishop Quinn and the many, many American Bishops who in my own experience have exemplified those words of the Pope, through friendship for scholars and firm support for their work. They make me believe that the vision of modern biblical scholarship contributing to the Church, described in the pages that follow, is not a dream but a possibility in our times.

The Critical Meaning of the Bible

Raymond E. Brown, S.S.

Geoffrey Chapman

Nihil Obstat:
Myles M. Bourke, S.S.L., S.T.D.
Censor Deputatus

Imprimatur:
Joseph T. O'Keefe
Vicar-General, *Archdiocese of New York*

Date:
June 29, 1981

The Nihil Obstat and Imprimatur are official declarations that a book or pamphlet is free of doctrinal or moral error. No implication is contained therein that those who have granted the Nihil Obstat and Imprimatur agree with the contents, opinions or statements expressed.

CASSELL LTD
35 Red Lion Square, London WCIR 4SG
and at Toronto
An affiliate of Macmillan Publishing Co., Inc.,
New York.

First published in Great Britain in 1982.

ISBN: 0 225 66325 2

Printed and bound in the
United States of America

CONTENTS

PREFACE

In the past five years I have devoted most of my efforts in applied scholarship to different facets of the issue I describe as *The Critical Meaning of the Bible,* a title that contains a deliberate play on the word "critical." Although the Bible is "of God," the biblical word was written by human beings. Consequently, the biblical books are subject to analysis such as one would use for determining the meaning of other ancient literature. This analysis is often referred to as "the critical method" or "biblical criticism." For some, the meaning derived through such biblical criticism is of purely scholarly concern with little applicability to modern religious issues—an attitude that has led many religious people to prefer a less sophisticated or even literalist approach to the Scriptures. I challenge this attitude, for I believe that a critical reading of the Bible is "critical" or crucial to the Churches and to thinking Christians.

In the judgment of most scholars biblical criticism is a correct (but not all-sufficient) approach to the Bible; and so, unless religious people and communities want a complete break with scholarship, they have little choice about working with the meaning of Scripture derived through this method. But the use of the critical method should be more than an unpleasant necessity; for when responsibly presented, the meaning derived thereby is not destructive. Rather it can be enormously helpful in challenging Christians and the Church(es), much as the prophets challenged Israel, and Jesus challenged the people of his time. A non-critical biblicism often tends to confirm the Church(es) and Christians in their *status quo* because the Bible so read yields what they have always thought it meant. Especially with regard to the NT, Bible-based Churches tend to use literalism to prove that they conform to the biblical directives for what the Church should be. Yet even an elementary study of history suggests that one should start with the opposite assumption, namely, that no twentieth-century Church is the same as the Church or Churches of NT times, and that inevitably twentieth-century Christians have a worldview different from that of first-century Christians. A critical study of the NT can point out unexpected differences, thus reminding us how much things have changed and what has been lost (or gained). True, one must avoid a naive romanticism that such a study will enable Christians to restore perfectly what once was. Nevertheless, Churches and Christians, confronted by a critical picture of NT times, can be led to needed reform, either by chopping away distracting accretions or by compensating for deficiencies.

What I have just described is not pure theory; that it is possible is verified by what has happened in Roman Catholicism in this century. Elsewhere (VCBRJ 3–11) I have suggested that history will divide this century roughly into thirds as regards the Roman Church's relation to the Bible. The first period (1900–1940) was dominated by the official Catholic rejection of modern biblical criticism because of fears that it would be destructive of doctrine. Eventually the Church learned what sooner or later all Churches learn—there is no way to avoid dealing with the results of responsible scholarship. Scholars can be purged once or twice, but a new generation keeps coming along; and eventually the Church has to enter into dialogue with them. Thus the second period (1940–70) saw the introduction of biblical criticism and the gradual but reluctant acceptance of its initial results in and through Vatican Council II. More than by any other single factor, the self-reform of Roman Catholicism in that Council was influenced by the modern approach to the Bible. Catholic mastery of biblical criticism has progressed since Vatican II, and the implications have proved more wide-ranging than even the most perceptive leaders of the Council foresaw. The third period of the century (1970–2000) in which we now live, therefore, has involved the painful assimilation of those implications for Catholic doctrine, theology, and practice.

The chapters in this volume are devoted to various aspects of that process; and, although composed separately, they have been woven together to give a consistent development of thought. (Sometimes, when there was previous publication, I have rewritten sections for greater continuity and as a more accurate expression of my thought.) At the beginning of each chapter I summarize in italics the theme of the chapter, relating its contents to the progression of thought in the volume.

Briefly, the book begins with an affirmation that, while the biblical "word of God" is inspired (and thus *of* God and not merely about Him), every *word* of it comes from human beings and is conditioned by their limitations. Because of the human element, one needs scientific, literary, and historical methods to determine what the ancient authors meant when they wrote—that knowledge does not come from revelation. But the meaning of the Bible as the Church's collection of sacred and normative books goes beyond what the authors *meant* in a particular book. Not only scholarship but also church tradition and teaching enters into the complex issue of what the Bible *means* to Christians. In this search for meaning there must be cooperation between scholars and church teachers, and two chapters are dedicated to that relationship and how it works. Even when cooperation is achieved and the issue of what the Bible means is clarified, how is that appropriated by the ordinary Christians into their thinking? This is discussed theoretically and then practically, using as an example the biblical picture of different priesthoods and what this can mean to believers today. Finally, what role does the modern critical understanding of the Bible have in the future of ecumenical relations among the various Churches? Again this is discussed both theoretically and practically, by settling on the example of different biblical understandings of episcopate.

Inevitably scholars tend to be excited by the meaning and importance of the field in which they work; but when that field is Bible, the word of God, there are grounds for believing that "meaning" and "importance" are more than self-delusion. I hope I can lead my readers to share my passionate conviction that critical biblical scholarship is not an option but a necessity, and that its results are critical for Christians, the Church, and the Churches.

Pentecost 1981

Chapter One
THE HUMAN WORD OF
THE ALMIGHTY GOD

Summary of the theme:[1] *The mystery of "the word of God" is appreciated only when we take both sides of that expression seriously. It is a human word, for God does not speak. But it is* OF *God, and not simply a human composition about God. The Bible makes us confront the seeming contradiction of a divine self-revelation in human terms.*

If the last one-third of the twentieth century is a period when we are seeking to assimilate the results of modern biblical criticism into Roman Catholic thought (and also into Christian thought in general—see Preface), it is not surprising that this assimilation is necessarily slow, even in academic areas. Biblical scholars themselves are continually developing insights in areas that affect theology;[2] and only now are we encountering a generation of Catholic theologians who were nurtured in their first studies on a critical approach to the

---

[1]The material represented in this chapter was originally delivered at Georgetown University, Washington, D.C. on Oct. 3, 1980, inaugurating the Theological Studies Lecture Series. It was printed in TS 42 (1981) 3–19, as " 'And the Lord Said'? Biblical Reflections on Scripture as the Word of God."

[2]There are areas that are only now being opened up (the different communities of the first century, and their different outlooks on christology, ecclesiology, eschatology, etc.) and there are areas that, in my judgment, have never been studied adequately (the different pneumatologies of the NT).

Bible, rather than appropriating it late in life and having to unlearn some of their early formation.[3] One feature of this gradual assimilation is that, while we may develop a sophisticated theology, we continue to use basic terms shaped in a precritical era without stopping to examine the meaning of those terms when rethought in a critical context. (Or even when those terms are rethought, often we do not reflect sufficiently on how they are understood by a noncritical audience for whom they may have a much simpler connotation.) In this chapter and the next I shall take the opportunity to rethink critically two basic tenets of the Catholic approach to the Bible, both of which were strongly affirmed at Vatican II, and both of which have serious implications for theology. The present chapter will concentrate on the implications of affirming that the Bible is the word of God, and the next chapter will discuss how one attains to the meaning of biblical passages and especially how the Church functions in "authentically interpreting the word of God."[4]

The terminology "the word of God," while a firm part of all Judeo-Christian thought, has in these last years been brought to the fore in Roman Catholicism in both liturgy and theology. In the vernacular Mass, as the passages of the lectionary are terminated, the lector proclaims, "This is the word of the Lord," to which all assent by the response, "Thanks be to God." And the Vatican II document on revelation, which was the subject of the battle that determined the direction of the Council and of Catholic theology in this century, was entitled *Dei verbum,* "The Word of God." Yet what does "word of God" mean when applied to the Bible? Are the Scriptures themselves the word of God or do they contain the word of God? In either case do we literally mean *word* of God? Does God speak? And if one smil-

---

[3]A biblical scholar must admire the industry of Schillebeeckx, who would take three years in middle age to do the exegetical reading that went into *Jesus* (New York: Seabury, 1979; see p. 36). But it is a commentary on Roman Catholic history in this century that such an endeavor had to be done in middle age and was not done in Schillebeeckx' theological training for the priesthood or even for the doctorate, as it would have been done in the case of a Protestant theologian like Pannenberg or Moltmann.

[4]Vatican II, *Dei verbum* 10: "The task of authentically interpreting the word of God, whether written or handed on, has been entrusted exclusively to the living teaching office of the Church. . . .This teaching office is not above the word of God but serves it."

ingly replies, "Not in the physical sense of emitting sound waves," there is still the question of whether God internally supplies words to the recipient of revelation and/or inspiration. I more than suspect that there are theologians who as good scholastics would not blanch at saying that technically God does not think, has never had an idea, and makes no judgments, but would hesitate at saying that God does not speak. Similarly, there are biblical interpreters who recognize anthropomorphism in biblical statements about God's smelling, walking, and begetting, but would hesitate about God's speaking.

Let me be precise about the limits of this discussion of the Bible as the word of God, lest I arouse misunderstanding or false expectation. First, I fully accept the Roman Catholic doctrine of the Bible as the word of God, and the whole discussion assumes that fact. This may disappoint those who think proof is needed that the Bible is the word *of God*—no such proof is possible beyond biblical self-claim and Church doctrine; it is a matter of faith. Catholics who are going through the struggle of faith may ask themselves why the biblical record written so long ago continues to have such a privileged position as a norm for Christian life, but in honesty I must say that the theoretical denial of the Bible as of truly divine origin is not a major problem in Catholic thought. On the North American scene there are a few left-wing Catholic theologians who regard the newspaper to be just as much a revelation of God's dealings with human beings as the Bible, but in my judgment that is more a problem in areas of Protestantism where liberalism has a long history. Catholic theologians of the left are a minority speaking to a minority; they have no following among the masses of Catholic faithful and will never influence the hierarchy nor change the Church.

The real struggle, which is between the Catholic center and the Catholic far-right, does not imperil the Catholic doctrine of the Bible as the word of God which both accept. In this instance, as in most others, the struggle concerns the *meaning* of the doctrine. It gets nasty only when the far-right claims that its understanding of the doctrine constitutes doctrine.[5] But if in this chapter I struggle with the

---

[5] In his speech at the Catholic University in Washington on Oct. 6, 1979, Pope John Paul II quoted his predecessor: "Among the rights of the faithful, one of the greatest is the right to receive God's word in all its entirety and purity." It is typical

difference between a centrist and a rightist understanding of the Bible as the word of God, it is not because I regard militant Catholic fundamentalism as a real threat. Rightist militancy is confined to a few Catholic newspapers and periodicals, more vocal than their numerical following justifies.[6] In smaller part, my debate has in mind the vast number of unconscious fundamentalists among Catholics who have little knowledge of the Bible and therefore make simple assumptions; it also has in mind the increasing number of conscious (but not militant) Catholic fundamentalists who have taken over Protestant fundamentalism from contacts in the charismatic or moral-issues movements.[7] In larger part, in a *theological* presentation I struggle over the Bible as word of God because I do not find that many theologians have been specific or clear on this subject, at least in a way that can reach a large audience of their coreligionists. I suspect that most modern Catholic theologians will agree with what follows and that some will even regard it as "old hat." Yet it is very difficult to find a theologian who writes specifically on whether God communicated directly in words (even internal words) in either biblical revelation or biblical inspiration. (The general affirmation that revelation is not propositional is not enough to settle the meaning of "the *word* of God.") This is no minor issue, because if God did not actually speak words (external or internal), one must admit clearly and firmly that every word pertaining to God in the history of the human race, including the biblical period, is a time-conditioned word, affected by limitations of human insight and problems. The attribution of a word to God, to Jesus, or to the Church would not enable that word to escape limitation.[8] The Roman Catholic Church has admitted that its past magisterial statements have been enunciat-

---

that many extreme rightists have quoted this as proof that the Pope wants *their* interpretations of Catholic doctrine presented. On this point, see Chapter Five below.

[6]For details see BRCFC 13; also Chapter Three below.

[7]I pass no judgment on such movements, but certainly biblical fundamentalism marks their Protestant components.

[8]This affirmation is sometimes translated hostilely as a denial of absolute truth. There is a God, and God is truth; and so there is absolute truth. The affirmation made above would mean only that every human perception of that truth is *partial*. The opposite affirmation would be that a human statement about God can be exhaustive.

ed in "the changeable conceptions of a given epoch."[9] Existentially that is a greater concession than saying that the Bible is phrased in the changeable conceptions of a given epoch,[10] but theologians who praise the Church's affirmation may ask themselves whether they have made explicitly and clearly a similar statement about the Bible.

If this chapter presses for theological frankness and clarity that will drive home inescapably the necessary point in the debate be tween the Catholic center and right, my contribution will be entirely from the vantage point of biblical criticism. I do not plan to consider the word of God philosophically (e.g., what human activities are possible to the Supreme Being) or in the context of historical theology (e.g., what various past church writers have thought about the word of God) or of systematic theology (e.g., whether there is a magisterial position or a unanimous theological position on what "the word of God" means).[11] Confining myself to an outlook gained from biblical criticism, however, may not be so modest an enterprise as it might first seem, for biblical critics are not of one mind on the question.[12] Let me illustrate this by quoting James Barr and Bernhard Anderson, two outstanding Christian OT scholars. Barr states: "My ac-

---

[9]*Mysterium ecclesiae*, a declaration of the Roman Doctrinal Congregation (1973); see the pertinent text in BRCFC 116–18.

[10]Theologically the Bible outranks magisterial statements (since no one claims they are the word of God); but existentially a Catholic moral theologian who disagreed with Qoheleth (Ecclesiastes) would be less likely to get in trouble than one who disagreed with *Humanae vitae*.

[11]In any case, it would be almost impossible to show that past writers or magisterial statements were dealing with the problem to be discussed here, for its particular nuance stems from modern biblical insights. Very interesting is the *sic et non* approach to dogmatic affirmations taken by Avery Dulles, "The Bible in the Church: Some Debated Questions," in *Scripture and the Charismatic Renewal,* ed. G. Martin (Milwaukee Symposiums; Ann Arbor: Servant, 1979) 5–27.

[12]What is described above is a discussion among centrists. Among Protestant evangelicals one may cite Harold Lindsell's works *The Battle for the Bible* (Grand Rapids: Zondervan, 1976) and *The Bible in the Balance* (1979)— works contradicted on a historical basis by J. Rogers and D. McKim, *The Authority and Interpretation of the Bible* (San Francisco: Harper & Row, 1979). Yet the latter work is too narrow in its own way, as shown at the 1980 AAR (Dallas) Meeting by Gerald T. Sheppard in the "Consultation on Evangelical Theology."

count of the formation of the biblical tradition is the account of a *human* work. . . . If one wants to use Word-of-God type language, the proper terms for the Bible would be Word of Israel, Word of some leading Christians."[13] Anderson responds: "The Word of God is not a voice carried on the sound waves, nor is it reducible to written form as a letter is dictated and transcribed. . . . Metaphor is an imaginative form of poetic speech in which one thing is spoken of as if it were the other. . . . Metaphorically, the Bible *is* the Word of God."[14]

If Anderson seems to be opposed diametrically to Barr, the "as if" in Anderson's statement needs to be probed. He continues:

> God chooses to use human literature, initially composed in the oral words of tradition and finally written down as Scripture, to establish relationship with people. . . . This Godly "use" of Scripture is an act of divine election. . . . The Bible, then, is a human medium, which God nevertheless uses authoritatively to speak to the believing and worshiping community. In this sense, the divine and the human are inseparably related in the Bible, making it impossible to separate Word of God and human words at any point. Of the canonical Scriptures it has been said in Chalcedonian language: *Omnia ex Deo, omnia ex hominibus.*

It is rather curious to find Anderson using Chalcedonian language to describe an adoptionistic approach to Scripture. Vatican II also used a christological model in attempting to understand Scripture, but one based on incarnation, not on adoption: "For the words of God, expressed in human language, have been made like human discourse, just as of old the Word of the eternal Father, when he took to himself the weak flesh of humanity, became like other men."[15]

The difference is significant, for many would judge that the word-of-God dimension is not properly represented by speaking of

[13] *The Bible in the Modern World* (New York: Harper & Row, 1973) 120.
[14] "The Bible in the Church Today," *Theology Today* 37 (1980) 4–5.
[15] *Dei verbum* 13.

the godly *use* of a human medium. Nevertheless, the simile of the pre-existent Word of God becoming flesh needs to be probed further in reflecting on how the Bible is the word of God. In a way, is this difference not related to the traditional Catholic distinction between revelation and inspiration in relation to the Bible? I say "Catholic distinction" because in some forms of Protestant thought that distinction seems to disappear, e.g., Carl Henry's statement, "The Bible is a propositional revelation of the unchanging Truth of God."[16] I say "traditional distinction" because some Catholics are moving away from it by collapsing inspiration into revelation. The traditional position has been that the whole Bible is inspired but only some parts of the Bible transmit revelation. But for Karl Rahner, God becomes the inspiring originator of the Scriptures by forming the apostolic Church and her constitutive elements, and the Bible is the literary objectification of a faith that is a response to revelation.[17] Avery Dulles states succinctly: "The Bible is a reliable, approved, canonical expression of the word of God; it not only transmits, but in some sense is, the word of God."[18] This language, which is faithful to Vatican II, leaves me wondering whether the distinction between transmitting and being the word of God is a way of rephrasing the revelation/inspiration issue. In any case, some theological theories do not adequately cover all parts of Scripture. To the jaundiced eye of a biblical scholar it often seems as if theologians phrase their theories of inspiration by reflecting on books like Genesis, the Gospels, and Romans; they might do better by trying their theories out on the first nine chapters of I Chronicles! To discuss thoroughly the Bible as word of God, one must face the problem that certain biblical authors were very conscious of having received a divine communication (the prophets, Paul) while other authors were not. Indeed, an author like Qoheleth would surely deny that he had received the word of God; he was writing out of collective human experience. Nevertheless, whether the lectionary reading be from Jeremiah, from Paul, or from Qoheleth, the Church would have it stated that this is the word of

---

[16]*God, Revelation and Authority* 3 (Waco: Word, 1979) 457.

[17]*Inspiration in the Bible* (New York: Herder and Herder, 1961; rev. 1964) esp. 50.

[18]"The Bible in the Church" 18; also "Scripture: Recent Protestant and Catholic Views," *Theology Today* 37 (1980) 7–26.

God. In attempting to deal with such problems, I shall treat under the heading of "revelation" biblical claims to receive or transmit the word of God,[19] and under the heading of "inspiration" the Church's understanding that the whole Bible is the word of God. In a way, then, I shall be dealing with realities reflected in the incarnational and adoptionistic approaches to the Bible described above.

BIBLICAL REVELATION AS WORD OF GOD

If we begin with the OT, the "Wisdom Books" make no claim to be the word of God,[20] nor do the songs we call Psalms. The two areas that need attention are the Prophets and the Law given to Moses; for in the biblical descriptions of the inaugural visions of the prophets and of Moses' vision on Sinai a divine word comes to man.[21]

The question of how to understand that divine word is already present in the oldest of the writing prophets. Amos 1:1 begins with "The words of Amos" *(Dibrê 'Amôs)*; it ends in 9:15 with "Thus says

---

[19]I make no attempt here at a definition of revelation. The self-disclosure of the God of mercy and love, delivering human beings from what enslaves them (oppression, sin, sickness, death) and making them His own in a special way (His people, His children), has found expression in various ways outside the Bible and in the Bible. If in dealing only with the latter, I concentrate here on the *word* of God, I acknowledge that the *actions* of God are equally and even primarily important in the Bible. *Dei verbum* made a great contribution to official Catholic thought by setting "deeds" alongside "words" in the description of revelation. The teaching of the Church is what gives me certitude that God has revealed Himself in the biblical actions and words. Granted that presupposition, biblical criticism can clarify that nonetheless the actions and words are fully human and subject to limitations.

[20]One exception is that in the self-description of divine Wisdom, she must be considered a type of divine word: "From the mouth of the Most High I came forth" (Sir 24:3). But that is chiefly through an identification of Wisdom and Law, and I plan to discuss the Law as a divine revelation.

[21]Although Moses can be described as prophet (Deut 18:15), in rabbinic tradition he is superior as the first of the prophets or the father of the prophets. While God spoke to both Moses and the prophets, the prophets saw Him through nine panes of glass or unclear glass, while Moses saw Him through only one pane of glass or clearer glass. See L. Ginzberg *The Legends of the Jews* 5 (Philadelphia: Jewish Publication Society, 1925) 404, n. 68; *Leviticus Rabba* 1.14.

the Lord your God" *('āmar YHWH 'Elōhêkā)*. If one may paraphrase the Esau/Jacob story, it sounds as if the voice is the voice of
God, but the words, the words of Amos. And all of this is more complicated for the biblical critic who thinks that 9:8–15 is an addendum
to Amos by a redactor who was not happy with the pessimistic tone
of many of the other "Thus says the Lord your God" passages in
Amos—one saying of the Lord God correcting another in the same
book. And, of course, that is even more deliberate when one com-
pares two different books. Because of political overuse, a word of the
Lord to Isaiah (2:1) is well known: "They shall beat their swords into
ploughshares, and their spears into pruning hooks" (Isa 2:4). Less familiar is the contradictory word that *the Lord speaks* to Joel: "Beat
your ploughshares into swords, and your pruning hooks into spears"
(Joel 4:10; RSV 3:10). One may argue whether God changes His
message according to circumstances, but it is hard to deny the likelihood that, in conveying a divinely received insight to a new generation, one prophet has deliberately taken the words of another
prophet and used them in a contrary way. The prophets leave no
doubt that they thought that God had communicated with them, but
they may have been more subtle than is often suspected about the
extent to which the words they uttered came from God.

Jeremiah offers the best opportunity to study this issue, precisely because his work is so self-reflective. On the one hand, we are told
that God put words into Jeremiah's mouth (1:9), and even that He
dictated to Jeremiah for writing purposes (36:1–4). Yet there is a
prose and poetic form of the same oracle (chaps. 7 and 26) which
betrays a certain freedom of expression. More important, there is a
series of complaints by Jeremiah that "the word of the Lord" that he
(Jeremiah) has spoken does not come to pass (17:15–16) and that he
has been deceived (15:18; 20:7, 9). There is revelation from God, for
Jeremiah's message is not of his own creation. But the phrasing of
the revelation seems to suffer from limitations. Once again I am
tempted by my paraphrase: the message is the message of God, but
the words are words of Jeremiah.

The question of whether a revealing God ever communicates in
words comes to a head in an OT perspective in the encounter between Moses and God on Sinai. In Jewish thought this was the su-

preme experience of God,[22] and its exalted status is reflected in the Johannine debate about whether Moses or Jesus has seen God (John 3:13). Christians were led to argue that Jesus had a contact with God that even went beyond that of Moses. And in modern Christian thought it continues to be poetically stated that if there was ever a time when the transcendent reached into the course of human history (from the outside rather than from within), it was on the two Mounts, Sinai and Calvary. Of course, the claims about what God said to Moses on Sinai can be presented in an inflated way that is easily discounted. (There is a rabbinic tendency to make even the later oral Law of the Mishnah part of the words of God to Moses.) In the second century of the common era, against those who took a literal view that every word or letter of the Law had a purpose,[23] Rabbi Ishmael defended the principle that "The Torah speaks the language of human beings."[24]

But let us move from the many casuistic parts of the Torah, which are clearly the product of collected jurisprudence, to the apodictic imperatives,[25] "Thou shalt" or "Thou shalt not," dealing with religious matters, where the speaker is portrayed as God. And indeed, let us concentrate on the Ten Commandments, which in Hebrew (unlike other commandments) are referred to as the "Ten Words" of God.[26] In theological tradition these have had a special place as reflecting the essence of what God demands of His people, and in modern biblical study they have been spoken of as the basic stipulations of the covenant between God and Israel. Are they really the words of God spoken (externally or internally) to Moses, or are they human formulations of a less specified revelation of divine moral demand? The modern biblical critic would be inclined to the latter

---

[22]Maimonides, *Guide to the Perplexed* 2.33, wrote of the Sinai event, "There never has been before nor will there ever be again anything like it."

[23]A similar view is found later in *Sanhedrin* 9a of the Babylonian Talmud: the whole Torah is from heaven, and not a single verse or letter can be attributed to Moses as if it were not uttered by God.

[24]See H. L. Strack, *Introduction to the Talmud and Midrash* (New York: Meridian, 1959; German 5th ed. 1920) 93–95.

[25]See JBC, art. 77 no. 87.

[26]This designation is preserved in the literal meaning of "Decalogue."

answer simply from a comparison of the two different forms of the Decalogue (Exod 20:1–17; Deut 5:6–21), especially since the *later*, Deuteronomic form of one commandment, separating the wife from the chattel and slaves, may represent a development of moral sensitivity.

But sometimes it is good to realize that modern biblical criticism is only rephrasing a problem recognized long before. In rabbinic discussions, how much was actually spoken by God and how much was phrased by Moses was very much an issue. In *Exodus Rabbah* 28.3 on Exod 19:8, God is portrayed as thinking, "When I say to them, 'I am the Lord your God,' they will ask, 'Who is speaking? God or Moses?' " Some rabbis thought that the people on the plain below heard the words of all ten commandments; but others asked which commandments were "given in the words of the Holy One" and which "by the hand of Moses." Maimonides, *Guide to the Perplexed* 2.33, argued that the people heard a sound but not the distinct words.[27] A common theory was that the people heard only the first two, understood as those in the first person: "I am the Lord your God" and "You shall not have other gods before me."[28] But at a later period Rabbi Mendel of Rymanóv suggested that all that was heard of the commandments was the first letter of the first word of the first commandment—the aleph of *'anōkî*, a soundless glottal stop! G. Scholem comments:

> With his daring statement that the actual revelation to Israel consisted only of the *aleph*, Rabbi Mendel transformed the revelation on Mount Sinai into a mystical revelation, pregnant with final meaning, but without specific meaning. . . . It has to be translated into human language, and that is what Moses did. In this light every statement on

---

[27]Maimonides thinks there was a divine "voice created for the purpose of speaking" the commandments.

[28]These "two" commandments cover the identity and unicity of God; in a subsequent commandment God refers to Himself in the third person: "You shall not take the name of the Lord your God in vain." See J. Z. Lauterbach, *Mekilta de-Rabbi Ishmael* 2 (Philadelphia: Jewish Publication Society, 1933) 228.

which authority is grounded would become a human interpretation, however valid and exalted, of something that
transcends it.[29]

I could phrase no better the issue I am raising of whether even
in the most sacred moments of revelation God communicates in
words.

Inevitably many Christians will look for a higher *form* of revelation in the NT.[30] Hebrews 1:1–2 comments: "On many occasions and
in many ways God spoke to the fathers by [in] the prophets; in these
last days He spoke to us by [in] the Son." This Jesus is the one who
dared to correct even the words God spoke to Moses: "You have
heard it said . . . but I say to you" (Matt 5:21 ff.). Yet in the words of
Jesus it is dubious that one encounters an unconditional, timeless
word spoken by God. The Son of God who speaks in the first three
Gospels is a Jew of the first third of the first century, who thinks in
the images of his time, speaks in the idiom of his time, and shares
much of the world view of his time. The Jesus of the Fourth Gospel,
who is pre-existent, does claim to have heard words in the presence
of his Father and to have brought them to earth (John 3:31–32; 5:30;
8:26, 40; 14:24; 15:15); but when one examines the words of the Johannine Jesus critically, they are often a variant form of the tradition
known in the Synoptics.[31] The very existence of diverse traditions of
the words of Jesus reflected in the four Gospels testifies to the fact
that his followers understood his words to be so time-conditioned
and so locale-conditioned as to require adaptation as they were trans-

---

[29]*On the Kabbala and Its Symbolism* (London: Routledge and Kegan Paul, 1965)
29–31. I am indebted to Rabbi Burton Visotzky of the Jewish Theological Seminary
(N.Y.C.) for help on some of these points.

[30]While the Christian view of revelation ascends from the prophets to Jesus, in the
Jewish view there is a descent from Moses to the prophets; and then after the prophets
ceased (I Macc 9:27; Ps 74:9) there was divine communication by the *bath qôl* and by
the holy spirit, with the latter being responsible for the non-prophetic portion of Scripture. See S. Lieberman, *Hellenism in Jewish Palestine* (New York: Jewish Theological
Seminary, 1950) 194–99; also Babylonian Talmud, *Megillah* 7a.

[31]See the evidence amassed by C. H. Dodd, *Historical Tradition in the Fourth Gospel* (Cambridge Univ. Press, 1963).

mitted to new times and places.[32] This is patent in Paul: although he cites the antidivorce statement of Jesus as coming from the Lord ("Not I, but the Lord": I Cor 7:10), he goes on to allow separation and perhaps even divorce in a situation that Jesus did not envisage ("I, not the Lord": 7:12).[33]

A special plea has sometimes been made for the unconditioned character of the words of the risen Jesus since he is one who has passed beyone space and time. Lack of limitation here would be quite important, for the sayings of the risen Jesus are often Church-foundational, involving apostleship, forgiveness of sins, baptism, conversion of the Gentiles, etc. Nevertheless, elsewhere[34] I have discussed the point that while these sayings are similar to each other in intent, they differ markedly from each other in actual wording, having much less similar vocabulary than parallel Synoptic sayings from the ministry.[35] Moreover, although theoretically these words were spoken in the early 30s, often there is little evidence that they influenced church life in the next few decades. For instance, in Acts 1:8 the risen Jesus tells his disciples that they will be his witnesses in Jerusalem, all Judea and Samaria, and to the ends of the earth. Yet when those developments occur in Acts, his disciples act as if they had never heard of such a directive (e.g., 8:14). The whole history of the Church in Acts reflects ignorance of the command of the risen Jesus in Matt 28:19 to make disciples *of all nations* (Acts 11:1–3; 15), baptizing them in the name of the Father, and of the Son, and of the

---

[32]This is now formally acknowledged in Catholic Church doctrine through the Instruction of the Roman Pontifical Biblical Commission on "The Historical Truth of the Gospels," which traces a process of adaptation during the formation of the Gospels. For the pertinent passages, see BRCFC 111–15.

[33]The antidivorce statement of Jesus is also modified when reported in Mark 10:11–12 (application to the wife) and in Matt 19:9 (the *porneia* exception)—modifications determined by the life situations of the communities which were diverse from that of Jesus.

[34]VCBRJ 107–8; also below p. 73.

[35]Some of them may be variants of ministry sayings; e.g., the postresurrectional "If you forgive men's sins, their sins are forgiven; if you hold them, they are held fast" (John 20:23) may be a variant of Matt 18:18, "Whatever you bind on earth will be bound in heaven; whatever you loose on earth will be loosed in heaven."

Holy Spirit (Acts 2:38; 8:16). What we seem to have is a communication by the risen Jesus that was only later vocalized in words as the various communities and writers came *post factum* to understand the import of the revelation.

The category of "speaking" may be an inadequate way to describe the unique, eschatological encounter with the risen Jesus—an approximation of this revelation to ordinary experience. If so, the study of the "words" of the risen Jesus (who has passed *beyond* the limitations of human circumstances) may confirm the thesis that only human beings speak words and that revelation by the word of God really means divine revelation to which human beings have given expression in words.

THE INSPIRED BIBLE AS WORD OF GOD

Although inspiration is sometimes thought to be a lower or less extraordinary charism than revelation (n. 30 above), the belief that only the Bible has been inspired by God has led that whole collection of books, composed over a period of a thousand years, to be called *simpliciter* "the word of God"—a designation covering even those books in which it is difficult to find any revelation at all. As Vatican Council I stated (DBS 3006), the books of Scripture "are held to be sacred and canonical . . . because they were written under the inspiration of the Holy Spirit." There have been many theories of inspiration: inspiration of the biblical authors (*Providentissimus Deus* of Pope Leo XIII); inspiration of the words; inspiration of the readers as they came to recognize God's work in the Scriptures; inspiration of the Church that gave birth to the NT (Karl Rahner). Such theories all touch on an aspect of the truth; however, they are scarcely adequate to answer all the problems detected by critical scholarship, e.g., the long history of composition that marked many works. These theories might explain how the final Gospels were inspired but do not cover Jesus the subject of the Gospels and the originator of the sayings preserved therein. Nor do they account sufficiently for the diversity that exists among biblical works, even among NT works, diversities so sharp that the biblical authors might not have agreed with one another on certain points.

Be all that as it may, my chief concern here is the extent to which the inspired Bible is a time-conditioned word, marked by the limitations of human utterance. Inevitably this brings up the sensitive question of inerrancy, for the tendency simply to equate inspiration and inerrancy implicitly denies human limitation to the biblical word of God. Without rehearsing the obvious, let me point out what can be learned from the increasing sophistication of official Catholic statements on this problem. Already in 1893 Pope Leo XIII in *Providentissimus Deus* (DBS 3288) excluded natural or scientific matters from biblical inerrancy, even if he did this through the expedient of insisting that statements made about nature according to ordinary appearances were not errors. (An example might involve the sun going around the earth.) While this understanding of error echoes an ancient equation of inerrancy with freedom from deception, it sounds strange to modern ears, for inculpable mistakes cease to be errors.[36] In any case, Pope Leo's approach undermined the very purpose for which most people want to stress inerrancy, namely, so that they can give unlimited confidence to biblical statements. The theory that these statements were made according to surface appearances and so are not necessarily correct from a scientific viewpoint is a backdoor way of admitting human conditioning on the part of the biblical authors.

Leo XIII stated (DBS 3290) that the same principles "will apply to cognate sciences, and especially to history," a concession that many thought opened the way to admitting that the biblical books were not necessarily historically accurate. Thirty years later Pope Benedict XV attempted to close this door in *Spiritus Paraclitus* (1920) when he stated that one could not apply universally to the historical portions of the Scriptures the principles that Leo XIII had laid down for scientific matters, namely, that the authors were writing only according to appearances (DBS 3653). Despite the respect that bound Catholic scholars to papal statements, this effort to save historical inerrancy failed, for the twentieth century produced indis-

---

[36]Of course, in saying that the biblical author spoke according to the ordinary natural appearances, one might be supposing that the author knew better but was simply adapting himself to the ignorance of the time. However, no serious scholar today could assume that the biblical authors had scientific or natural knowledge beyond that of their times.

putable evidence of historical inaccuracies in the Bible.[37] It was no surprise, then, that when inerrancy was discussed at Vatican II, no less a figure than Cardinal Koenig could dare to read off a list of historical errors in the Bible and to affirm that "the Biblical Books are deficient in accuracy as regards both historical and scientific matters."[38] In questioning the historical inerrancy of the Bible, Catholic scholars had worked upon a good philosophical principle, *Ab esse ad posse valet illatio:* if historical errors exist, they must be possible.

But all this development left untouched an area that even some Protestant discussions of inerrancy had avoided. It is one thing to admit that the biblical writers were limited in their knowledge of science and history. It is another thing to admit that the biblical writers had religious limitations. The Bible, most would recognize, was not written as a scientific or historical textbook, but many would think of it as almost a religious textbook. Nevertheless, critical investigation points to religious limitations and even errors. For instance, many recognize that Job 14:13–22 and Sir 14:16–17; 17:22–23; 38:21 deny an afterlife. It is not that the respective authors were ignorant of the possibility of an afterlife; they brought it up as a solution and rejected it at the same time that other biblical authors were accepting it. If one accepts the afterlife teaching of Jesus (which was harmonious with Pharisaic Judaism), how does one reconcile a word of God in Job that seems contradictory to a word of God spoken by Jesus? Leaving aside the possibility of excising the Job passage from the Bible,[39] believers are faced with two possibilities.

1) If one has an *a priori* view of inerrancy that forbids a religious error in the Bible, one will have to argue insistently that Job

---

[37]For instance, the discovery of the Neo-Babylonian chronicles made it lucidly clear that the dates assigned to various Babylonian interventions in Daniel were wrong; no longer could exegetes say that those dates might be true because of our ignorance of Babylonian chronology. One may very well answer that the author of Daniel was not writing history, but surely he used those dates because he thought they were correct.

[38]A. Grillmeier, "Dogmatic Constitution on Divine Revelation, Chapter III," in *Commentary on the Documents of Vatican II,* ed. H. Vorgrimler (New York: Herder and Herder, 1969) 3. 205.

[39]Excision may seem a fantastic solution, but the canon-within-the-canon approach virtually excises passages deemed theologically unworthy by marginalizing them.

did not mean what he seems to say. A great deal of time and effort has been spent by interpreters in such efforts, whether applied to religious errors or to the above-mentioned historical and scientific errors. This approach, in my judgment, is an unmitigated disaster, draining off energy into the creation of ingenious implausibilities and turning exegesis into apologetics. A recent book by Paul Achtemeier[40] documents the bankruptcy of this method in Protestantism. It is sad that simultaneously the ultraconservative Catholic *Homiletic and Pastoral Review* was in its November 1979 issue publishing an article by a convert, Edith Black, entitled "Inerrancy in the Bible," which seeks (by a literalist interpretation of church documents) to introduce into Catholicism a fundamentalist view of inerrancy similar to that which has vitiated the sincere efforts of Protestant evangelicals. It has been said that after Vatican II Catholics seem intent to duplicate in a decade the mistakes that Protestants took centuries to make. That holds not only for liberal excesses but also for ultraconservative ones.

2) One can be more modest in making *a priori* claims about what the God who inspired the Scriptures will tolerate by way of error. (It remains a paradox that we worship a God whose thoughts are not our thoughts, and yet we tend to be so sure about what He would think fitting. Every clearly discernible action of His has been a surprise; how can we be so sure what He must do?) This means that we shift to an *a posteriori* approach to inerrancy. Using the best biblical methods available, scholars seek to determine what the human author meant with all his limitations. Combining this with a belief in inspiration, they recognize that there is a *kenōsis* involved in God's committing His message to human words. It was not only in the career of Jesus that the divine has taken on the form of a servant (Philip 2:7). If one discovers religious errors, one does not seek to explain them away; one recognizes that God is willing to work with human beings in all their limitations, and that each author's contribution is only part of a larger presentation of biblical truth. In one of his Lincolnesque asides, Avery Dulles has said about eucharistic practice that sometimes we spend too much effort in protecting Jesus from

---

[40]*The Inspiration of Scripture: Problems and Proposals* (Philadelphia: Westminster, 1980).

things Jesus might not wish to be protected from. We have spent too much time protecting the God who inspired the Scriptures from limitations that He seems not to have been concerned about. The impassioned debate about inerrancy tells us less about divine omnipotence (which presumably allows God to be relaxed) than about our own insecurity in looking for absolute answers.

Many of us think that at Vatican II the Catholic Church "turned the corner" in the inerrancy question by moving from the *a priori* toward the *a posteriori* in the statement of *Dei verbum* 11: "The Books of Scripture must be acknowledged as teaching firmly, faithfully, and without error that truth which God wanted put into the sacred writings for the sake of our salvation." Within its context, the statement is not without an ambiguity that stems from the compromise nature of *Dei verbum*. The Council in 1962 rejected the ultraconservative schema "On the Sources of Revelation" that originally had been submitted, and so it became a matter of face-saving that in the revisions and in the final form of the Constitution the ultraconservatives should have their say. The result is often a juxtaposition of conservative older formulations with more open recent formulations. Those who wish to read *Dei verbum* in a minimalist way can point out that the sentence immediately preceding the one I just quoted says that everything in Scripture is asserted by the Holy Spirit and can argue that therefore "what God wanted put into the Scripture for the sake of our salvation" (which is without error) means every view the human author expressed in Scripture. However, there is noncritical exegesis of Church documents as well as noncritical exegesis of Scripture.[41] Consequently, to determine the real meaning of

---

[41]Essential to a critical interpretation of church documents is the realization that the Roman Catholic Church does not change her official stance in a blunt way. Past statements are not rejected but are requoted with praise and then reinterpreted at the same time. It is falsely claimed that there has been no change towards the Bible in Catholic Church thought because Pius XII and Vatican II paid homage to documents issued by Leo XIII, Pius X, and Benedict XV and therefore clearly meant to reinforce the teaching of their predecessors. What really was going on was an attempt gracefully to retain what was salvageable from the past and to move in a new direction with as little friction as possible. To those for whom it is a doctrinal issue that the Church never changes, one must repeat Galileo's *sotto voce* response when told that it was a doctrinal issue that the earth does not move: "E pur si muove" ("Nevertheless, it

Dei verbum one must study the discussions in the Council that produced it, and one must comb a body of evidence that can be read in
different ways.[42] A change of direction is detectable in the fact that
the term "inerrancy" was dropped from the Constitution, and that
the final statement about error came after Cardinal Koenig and others had pointed out the kinds of errors that do exist in Scripture. As
Grillmeier has observed, without confining the inerrancy of Scripture to matters of faith and morals (a formulation condemned in earlier Roman statements), "the Theological Commission—as well as
clearly emphasizing the universal extent of inspiration—keeps the
way open for a new interpretation of inerrancy."[43] It does this by relating the truth of the Scriptures to the salvific purpose for which
God intended the Scriptures. It is not as if some parts of Scripture
teach without error "truth for the sake of salvation," and other parts
do not. Everything in Scripture is inerrant to the extent to which it
conforms to the salvific purpose of God.

Thus in the inerrancy question Vatican II assumes as *a priori*
that God wants the salvation of His people. The extent to which
truth in Scripture conforms to that purpose is an *a posteriori* issue.
And in determining that, I would contend that one cannot be satis-
fied with the literal meaning of Scripture, i.e., with what the human
authors intended,[44] as deciphered by historical criticism. A great mis-
take in dealing with inerrancy has been to take an ancient principle
that the Bible contains God's truth and to apply that principle in
terms of the exclusively dominant literal sense—a modern approach
to the Bible. The human author of Job made an error in denying an

---

moves"). And the best proof of movement is the kind of biblical scholarship practiced
by ninety-five percent of Catholics writing today, a kind of scholarship that would not
have been tolerated for a moment by church authorities in the first forty years of this
century.

[42]The evidence is given and interpreted in the Grillmeier article cited in n. 38
above. A much more conservative interpretation is offered by A. Bea, *The Word of
God and Mankind* (Chicago: Franciscan Herald, 1967) 184–93. Cardinal Bea never
mentions Cardinal Koenig's speech which seemingly did not agree with Bea's position
that even historical background is presented in the Bible without error. See below p.
67.

[43]Ibid. 214

[44]In the next chapter we shall see that the literal sense is larger than the author's
intent, covering sources and redaction.

afterlife. But the meaning of Job as a biblical book goes beyond what its author intended, for Job became a *biblical* book not when it was written but when it was joined to other books as part of the Bible. First it became part of the sacred collection of Israel and was joined in Babylonian and Palestinian Judaism to the apocalyptic material in Isaiah (26:19) and Daniel (12:2), which maintained a doctrine of resurrection; and in Egyptian Judaism it was joined to II Maccabees and Wisdom, which offered other views of the afterlife. Finally, Job was joined in Christianity to a NT which was unanimous in its affirmation of an afterlife. This joining relativized the position of Job, so that as part of the canonical collection the author's rejection of an afterlife could be seen as a step in the gradual perception of a larger truth. (As I insist in the next chapter, however, that larger view should not silence Job's protest against resorting to an afterlife as a solution for all the problems of justice—inadequate in one way, it remains a voice of conscience in another.)

But even the placing of a book in the Bible does not tell us fully about its meaning. For this Bible to be normative for Christian life, it has had to be accepted by the Church and proclaimed as part of a living tradition in the community of believers.[45] "Biblical meaning" is not simply what a passage meant to the author who wrote it (literal meaning), or what it meant to those who first accepted it into a normative collection (canonical meaning); biblical meaning is also what the passage means today in the context of the Christian Church. And when one speaks of the Bible "teaching without error that truth which God put into the Scripture for the sake of our salvation," one is speaking of biblical meaning as a whole and not of an isolated stage of that meaning. It is for that reason that I have conceived this chapter on the word of God as intimately related to the next chapter on the relation of the literal sense of Scripture (discovered by historical criticism) to other senses of Scripture and on the role of the Church in interpreting Scripture.

But in the limited context here I have argued that inerrancy cannot be applied *a priori* to the literal sense of Scripture in a way that would free it from human limitation. Thus, whether the words

---

[45]I write as a Christian; a Jew might choose to phrase this in terms of rabbinic tradition.

of the Bible reflect revelation received from God or constitute an account inspired by God, they remain very much human words, reflecting partial insight and time-conditioned vision. A perceptive book written some twenty years ago by Jean Levie dealt with some of the problems I have considered under the title *The Bible: Word of God in Words of Men.*[46] While at the time one needed the emphasis in that title for pedagogical purposes, to speak of "word of God in words of men" is tautological. Only human beings use words; and so, when one has entitled divine communication "word of God," one has already indicated that the divine communication is in human words,[47] and therefore that the communication is in a time-conditioned and limited form.

*   *   *

As indicated at the start, I have spelled this out because, while I think that most centrist Catholic theologians agree with me, they may not have been sufficiently clear at a time when "word of God" is still likely to be understood simplistically by most Catholics. Nevertheless, I am conscious that my emphasis on the "word" section of "word of God" has not allowed equal time for the "of God" part which, as I said, I have assumed throughout. The fact that the "word" of the Bible is human and time-conditioned makes it no less "of God." In the Bible God communicates Himself to the extraordinary extent that one cay say that there is something "of God" in the words. All other works, patristic, Thomistic, and ecclesiastic, are words *about* God; only the Bible is the word *of* God.[48] If I may re-

---

[46](New York: Kenedy, 1961). The French title was more perceptive: *Parole humaine et message de Dieu* (Paris: Desclée de Brouwer, 1959).

[47]If it is objected that "word of God" is also a title for the Second Person of the Trinity, I would reply that it is a title given to that Person alone who took to Himself the human, the time-conditioned, and the limited.

[48]J. Ratzinger, in *Commentary on the Documents of Vatican II* 3 (n. 38 above) 194: "It is important to note that [in *Dei verbum* 9] only Scripture is defined in terms of what *is*: it is stated that Scripture *is* the word of God consigned to writing. Tradition, however, is described only functionally, in terms of what it *does:* it hands on the word of God, but *is* not the word of God." This unique status of Scripture explains the last sentence in n. 4 above.

turn to the christological comparison with which I began, Jesus as "fully divine and fully human" has been rejected not only consciously by nonbelievers but also unconsciously by believers. The nonbeliever regards the fully divine as incompatible with the human; the believer often regards the fully human as incompatible with the divine. To the biblical exception to the full humanity of Jesus ("without sinning" in Heb 4:15) are sometimes added "without ignorance," "without temptation," and "without limitation of world view." Consequently, if another Christian, who believes in the divinity of Jesus, insists that Jesus did not know all things, did not foresee the distant future, and was tempted, having to learn obedience, christological fundamentalists will accuse that person of denying that Jesus is the Son of God. Small wonder that if a believer in revelation and inspiration insists that the biblical word is human, time-conditioned, and subject to limitation and error, biblical fundamentalists will accuse that person of denying that the Bible is the word of God. This chapter has been dedicated to the thesis that only a believer who insists on such limitations holds that the Bible is the *word* of God.

St. John Chrysostom recognized what was involved when he wrote that it was "for the sake of our salvation" that God expressed Himself in the Scriptures where "the ordinariness of the words is made necessary by our limitations."[49] And it was Chrysostom that Vatican II had in mind when it taught (*Dei verbum* 13): "The words of God, expressed in human language, have been made like to human discourse, just as of old the Word of the eternal Father, having taken to himself the weak flesh of humanity, became like other human beings."[50]

---

[49]*Homily on Genesis* PG 53, 135A. See R. C. Hill, "St. John Chrysostom and the Incarnation of the Word in Scripture," *Compass Theology Review* 14 (1980) 34–38.

[50]Just before these words *Dei verbum* quotes his *Homily on Genesis* PG 53, 134.

Chapter Two
WHAT THE BIBLICAL
WORD MEANT
AND WHAT IT MEANS

Summary of the theme:[1] *Books written by limited human beings in the language and outlook of their times have been gathered into the Bible which is held in faith to be God's word for all times. We cannot bypass historical criticism which is concerned with what a passage meant to the author who wrote it, but the meaning of the Bible goes beyond that. The Bible ceases to be an instrument of comfortable self-affirmation for Christians and the Church when we recognize the tensions between what the word meant and what it means.*

We have now seen that *word* of God (since God does not really speak in words) means a divine communication in human words spoken and written by people who had limited knowledge and restricted worldview and were facing specific problems. Granted such limitations, how does the meaning they intended relate to the normative role of the Bible in the Church? The answer to this question involves a consideration both of hermeneutical (or meaning) issues and of the role of church authority in discerning the meaning of

---

[1]The material represented in this chapter originally constituted the Twenty-Fifth Annual Robert Cardinal Bellarmine Lecture, delivered at St. Louis University on Oct. 15, 1980, and printed in TD 28 (Winter 1980) 305–19 as "The Meaning of the Bible."

Scripture. I shall devote half of a chapter to each of these two consid-
erations; but before I begin, let me recall official Catholic statements
on both issues. In *Divino Afflante Spiritu* (DBS 3826) Pope Pius XII
affirmed clearly the primacy of the literal sense: "The foremost and
greatest endeavor of the interpreters should be to discern and define
that sense of the biblical words which is called literal . . . so that the
mind of the author may be made abundantly clear." And *Dei verbum*
(10) of Vatican Council II states, "The task of authentically interpreting the word of God, whether written or handed on, has been entrusted exclusively to the living teaching office of the Church, where
authority is exercised in the name of Jesus Christ."

WHAT THE BIBLE MEANT

The above-cited equation of the literal sense with what the author intended may be too narrow, as will be discussed below. But
certainly the author's intent is a major factor in a literal sense that is
detected by the historical-critical method developed in the last one
hundred years. The pope's insistence that such a meaning and such a
method constitute "the foremost and greatest endeavor of interpreters" is not universally accepted. Indeed, some would regard it as a
very dubious endeavor. Let me survey the different scholarly or religious reasons that lead people to an unappreciative attitude toward
the literal meaning of the Bible as diagnosed by the historical-critical
method:

(1) Some liberals regard the quest for the literal sense as the
correct approach to the Bible, but not very important, simply because the Bible is not very important. In their judgment the Bible
represents a phase in the history of religion, and some modern theological factor may be far more important in determining a correct
stance than is an antiquated voice from the past.

(2) From an opposite viewpoint, some who regard the Bible as
their complete source of spirituality or religion find sterility in the
historical-critical quest for the literal sense. The meaning thus uncovered is often not particularly elevating or spiritual, and sometimes it has little apparent applicability to modern needs. With
qualifications I would place in this category Walter Wink's famous

charge that the historical-critical method is bankrupt.[2] This charge has been taken up by Reginald Fuller[3] who states that the bankruptcy of the historical-critical method should be overcome by feedback received from the believing community. However, George Landes[4] has perceptively challenged Wink's assertion: "What is bankrupt is not the method itself, but the attempt to make it serve purposes it was not intended to serve." And rhetorically I would wish to ask Fuller what is there in the nature of the historical-critical method that should ever have prevented its practitioners from being members of the believing community, and is he not blaming a method for the prejudices of some who employ it. It is true that, as a child of the post-Enlightenment, biblical criticism has tended to be almost doctrinaire in its skepticism about the transcendent, e.g., in ruling out of court any evidence that Jesus worked miracles. There has also been a tendency to regard as unscientific any interest in what the texts meant religiously to the people who wrote them. But it is time that we identify such prejudices as regrettable accretions rather than as intrinsic principles of the method.

(3) Some object to the historical-critical quest as too pretentious, uncovering a sense of the Bible but not the most important meaning. They appreciate more the spiritual sense, or canonical sense, or theological sense, or literary sense. I shall discuss this approach in detail below; for the moment I simply remark that, in evaluating it, one must pay close attention to whether it makes the literal sense a major or minor factor in a larger picture.

(4) Some reject the historical-critical method as theologically dangerous. We may distinguish here two different attitudes: (a) One theological objection (encountered among conservative circles, both Protestant and Catholic) is that the quest for what the human author intended treats the Bible as if it were not the word *of God*. When the historical-critical method uncovers the limitations and shortcomings in the author's religious views, that is seen as a blasphemous denial

---

[2] *The Bible in Human Transformation* (Philadelphia: Fortress, 1973) 1.

[3] "What Is Happening in New Testament Studies?" *St. Luke's Journal of Theology* 23 (1980) 96.

[4] *Journal for the Study of the Old Testament* 16 (1980) 33.

of the claim that God has spoken. Chapter One was dedicated precisely to the rejection of such an approach which really denies that the Bible is the *word* of God. (b) Another theological objection (most often encountered among Catholic conservatives) flows from the fact that the literal sense uncovered by the historical-critical method often does not agree with the way in which the Church has interpreted a passage. Since they accept the Church's interpretation, they reject the exegetical method as false and dangerous. The second half of this chapter will be devoted to that issue.

But before I move away from this catalogue of disparagements of the historical-critical method, let me comment on two attitudes that I find among some Roman Catholics. Too often one hears the glib assertion that the Church and Christians read the Bible without the historical-critical method for 1700 years and therefore it cannot be an essential method. The rejection of the necessity of employing new intellectual tools on the grounds that one's predecessors did not have them has been encountered over and over again in Christian history, e.g., in the early centuries the resistance to the introduction of formal philosophy into Christian theology; in the Middle Ages the condemnation of Aquinas' attempts to import Aristotelianism into theology; in modern times the resistance to information derived from natural sciences, psychology, and sociology. It is one thing not to use a method when it has not been discovered and no one else is using it. But to refuse the historical-critical method now when it has become part of the modern approach to all other literature is tantamount to a theological statement denying the human element in the word of God. It removes the biblical authors from the world of ordinary experience with its limitations. The decision *against* the historical-critical method, even under the guise of a sophisticated appreciation of the history of exegesis, is a form of theological fundamentalism.[5]

A second attitude among some Roman Catholics is that historical-critical exegesis is being overused and abused by their fellow-religionists. Extreme caution is required here. There are a number of

---

[5] I have no objection to the contention that the historical-critical approach is not the whole of exegesis, but only to those who substantially reject the literal sense. See the discussion by D. C. Steinmetz, "The Superiority of Pre-Critical Exegesis," *Theology Today* 37 (1980) 27–38.

scholars, particularly among the French, who distinguished themselves in the difficult days before Vatican II by adopting a mildly critical approach to the Bible and by using that to construct a biblical theology, the very richness of which served as an apologetic for a more open stance by the Church toward biblical criticism. But when after Vatican II another generation of scholars pursued the critical issues in a much more "hard-nosed" way, the hitherto appreciated work of the older generation now began to be criticized as uncritical and not "up-to-date." Such criticisms left their wound, and famous "names" of the early 1960s have sometimes aligned themselves with ultraconservative positions and with expressions of fear about the future. Alas, it is often a case of there being none more conservative than the old liberal whose time has passed and who thought that he knew exactly how far progress would go. But while one can understand this human drama, firmness is required in pointing out that some of the Catholic scholars most vociferous in their attacks on biblical criticism and Catholic critics are people whose own work has been judged as quite inadequate.

Let me give as an example a contemporary assailant on the American scene who has been quite blunt. Manuel Miguens has devoted much of his writing career in these last years to attacking fellow Catholic scholars for the dangers he sees in their application of biblical criticism to early Christian ecclesiology, christology, and mariology. In a recent issue of *Communio* (7 [1980] 24–54) he was severe on such biblical criticism as a threat to the Gospel; but in evaluating this attitude, judgments upon Miguens' own ability to understand and practice biblical criticism should be remembered. His book *Church Ministries in New Testament Times* (Arlington, Va.: Christian Culture Press, 1976) was reviewed in CBQ (40 [1978] 130–31) by J. H. Elliott of the University of San Francisco: "I cannot in good conscience recommend this work. . . .It reflects an awareness neither of the current *status quaestionis* of this complex issue nor of the main research involved. The historicity of texts and the unbiasedness of the biblical authors are accepted with uncritical credulity. Exegetical and historical problems are dismissed as fabrications produced by 'modern fashions and moods in scholarship.' " Another book by Miguens, *The Virgin Birth: An Evaluation of Scriptural Evidence* (Westminster, Md.: Christian Classics Inc., 1975) was reviewed by the

Lutheran scholar Karl Donfried of Smith College in TS (38 [1977] 160–62): "While at points raising significant questions and suggesting viable exegetical possibilities, this is, on the whole, a very uncautious book which is bound to mislead many naive readers. Under cover of academic biblical respectability, it abounds in incomplete and inaccurate exegesis and unwarranted generalizations. The real methodology employed is not that of exegesis but of eisegesis." A Catholic scholar's judgment on the same book of Miguens was recorded by Stanley Marrow of Weston School of Theology in CBQ (38 [1976] 576–77): "The literary genre of this monograph can best be described as polemical exegesis. But to the present reviewer, the exegesis is faulty and the polemic wide of the mark." Marrow warns, "What militates most against the proper evaluation of the Scriptural evidence, however, is the fact that the exegesis is not *voraussetzungslos* [without presuppositions], in that it presupposes its own outcome from the start."

By way of personal comment let me state firmly that I regard as ridiculous the charge that biblical criticism is now being overused in Roman Catholicism. Catholic scholars have been permitted to use criticism for no more than one-third of a century, and indeed its implications are only now being appropriated.[6] We have produced full-scale commentaries on very few books of the Bible. We are still struggling with giving our people even an elementary knowledge of the Bible as it is understood in scholarship. Critical biblical thought has had relatively little impact on some leading theologians whose scriptural views were shaped in the Catholicism of a pre-critical period. There has been no evidence of a major impact of critical biblical thought upon Roman statements. To Catholics who express fears about biblical criticism, one may well reply in the crude argot of the street: "Don't knock it till you've tried it."[7] And I would add to that maxim "—tried it and been judged by your fellow-scholars as knowing what you are doing." In my judgment the use of the historical-critical method is not simply an option but a necessity, because, when practiced by believers, it involves a fundamental theological

---

[6]Chapter Four below will examine the slowness of the impact of NT scholarship on the Church.

[7]See my warning on this in JBC, art. 77, #24.

statement about the *word* of God as always conditioned by time and place and circumstance, and yet truly "of God." Despite their different agenda ultraliberals and ultraconservatives can agree that the historical-critical method leads to denying the "of God" in favor of the human "word" element, but that may well be because neither group can accept an incarnational theology of the fully divine in the fully human.

VARIOUS BIBLICAL SENSES

I have made this point strongly so that my further remarks about the inadequacy of the quest for the literal sense cannot be understood as denigrating the importance of that quest. In suggesting that what is grasped through the historical-critical method is not the whole meaning of the Bible, I am in good company among exegetes and theologians today.[8] However, I am not jumping upon any bandwagon; for such an approach has marked my own academic career from the very beginning, as illustrated in my interest in the *sensus plenior* of Scripture.[9] I have returned to that interest from time to time,[10] although I recognized quickly that, formulated in terms of the *sensus plenior,* the hermeneutic stress that I advocated was too narrowly scholastic and tied into the principle of single authorship for a biblical book.[11] Moreover, in the 1950s and 1960s it was not the *sensus plenior* that needed emphasis in Roman Catholicism but the pri-

---

[8]J. A. Sanders, *Torah and Canon* (Philadelphia: Fortress, 1972); H. Frei, *The Eclipse of Biblical Narrative* (New Haven: Yale, 1974); G. T. Sheppard, "Canon Criticism: The Proposal of Brevard Childs and an Assessment for Evangelical Hermeneutics," *Studia Biblica et Theologica* 4 (1974) 3–17; also his *Wisdom as a Hermeneutical Construct* (BZAW 151; Berlin: de Gruyter, 1980) on "canon conscious redactions" and his article "Canonization" in *Interpretation* 36 (1982); B. S. Childs, *Biblical Theology in Crisis* (Philadelphia: Westminster, 1970); also his *Introduction to the Old Testament as Scripture* (Philadelphia: Fortress, 1979) esp. 72ff.; P. Stuhlmacher, *Historical Criticism and Theological Interpretation* (Philadelphia: Fortress, 1977).

[9]CBQ 15 (1953) 141–62; also *The Sensus Plenior of Sacred Scripture* (Baltimore: St. Mary's Univ., 1955).

[10]CBQ 25 (1963) 262–85; ETL 43 (1967) 460–69; JBC art. 71, esp. ##56–70.

[11]Perceptively J. M. Robinson, CBQ 27 (1965) 6–27, saw beneath the scholastic dress and related the quest for the *sensus plenior* to the problems of the new hermeneutic.

macy of the literal sense, lest the challenge of the biblical authors be relativized and not bring about the appropriate change in Catholic attitudes.

Before going beyond the literal sense, let me first comment that the equation of the literal sense with what the (final) human author intended is too narrow. A quest conducted by the historical-critical method employs form criticism, source criticism, redaction criticism, audience criticism, etc. Applying these to the Gospels, for instance, one would investigate what Jesus meant when he did or said something (if recoverable); how that was shaped in the apostolic preaching and precanonical source (both as to meaning and form); what Mark meant when he incorporated this earlier tradition into his Gospel and used it to answer religious problems in the community he addressed; and further (if applicable) what Matthew and Luke meant when they rewrote the Marcan tradition, at times correcting the Marcan emphasis. Under the rubric of the literal sense one would also have to include the intentions of the redactor. For instance, the Fourth Evangelist, responsible for most of John, had his own meaning; but sometimes that was modified by additions of passages representing the work of a redactor—the literal sense would involve both meanings. An even more dramatic example is found in the Book of Isaiah where one must take into account not simply what Proto-Isaiah meant but how his work was modified through the additions of Deutero-Isaiah and Trito-Isaiah. A commentator must never fail to give attention to the sense a passage has in a book taken as a whole.[12]

In my judgment we go beyond the literal sense when we move from the meaning of the book in itself to the meaning that the book has when it is joined to other books in the canon of Scripture. For the books of the Hebrew Scriptures (so far as Christians are concerned), incorporation into a canon would have a double perspective:

---

[12]I should caution here that some would already speak of this as "canonical criticism." I object strongly to removing the sense of a whole book from the literal sense, because that would reduce the literal sense to the meaning of non-existent sources. No matter how certain our conclusions may be, Proto-, Deutero-, and Trito-Isaiah are reconstructions; the only extant literature is the *Book* of Isaiah, and the literal sense is the sense of that book. On the borderline between the literal and the canonical senses are additions made by a final redactor in order to harmonize a book with other sacred books. This resembles Sheppard's "canon conscious redactions."

when they became part of the collection we call Old Testament, and when that collection was modified through the addition of the New Testament. Let me illustrate this "canonical sense" of Scripture. The joining of Deutero-Pauline works (the Pastorals, Ephesians, perhaps Colossians and II Thessalonians) to the indisputably genuine Pauline writings means that we have a larger view of how the Pauline theology developed and was adapted. (This was not necessarily a smooth and harmonious adaptation; at times it involved correction, albeit benevolent, of what were seen by the end of the first century to be Pauline lacunae or even exaggerations.) In Chapter One I pointed out how the rejection of an afterlife by Job is modified when Job is included in an OT canon that contains affirmations of resurrection or other forms of afterlife (Isaiah 26; Daniel; Wisdom; II Maccabees) and is modified even more when joined to a NT that is unanimous in its affirmation of an afterlife. Some of the adaptations caused by the presence of a book in a canon are more subtle. Interpreters of the NT can scarcely avoid thinking of Luke as a Gospel and comparing it to Mark and Matthew; in part that is because in the canonical process Luke was separated from Acts and placed in the midst of three other "Gospels." But this may represent a serious qualification of Luke's intention. The man we call "Luke" not only modified Mark in composing the work we call "Luke"; he also accompanied the story of Jesus with a story of the Church called "Acts." Presumably that was because he did not feel that one could do justice to God's revelation and plan simply by telling the story of Jesus without an explicit account of what the Spirit and the apostles did. The canonical process has, in a sense, undone his intent.

Let me show the implication of the canonical sense for a specific theological point. A work done jointly by Roman Catholics and Protestants, *Mary in the New Testament,*[13] acknowledged that it is extremely difficult to be sure that a Mary/Eve parallelism was the literal sense (author's intent) in the accounts of the mother of Jesus in John 2 and 19 and of the woman who gives birth to the messianic child in Revelation 12. But the *Mary* volume continued, "When John and Revelation are put in the same canon, a catalytic action may occur, so that the two women are brought together and the parallelism

---

[13]Edited by R.E. Brown *et al.* (New York: Paulist 1978) 30–31.

to Eve becomes more probable." In TS (40 [1979] 539) Neil J. Mc-
Eleney, a Catholic scholar, criticized this approach strongly: "The
book concedes too much to 'canonical criticism.' Unless one allows
biblical inspiration to the act of assembling the NT canon, any 'catalytic action' [?] would not result in a biblical meaning inherent in the
text but would be eisegesis or, in a kinder view, theologizing upon
the text." If one lays aside the issue of inspiration which is a dubious
distraction in relation to this question,[14] McEleney is denying that a
meaning that surfaces *after* books are placed in the canonical collection is a "biblical meaning"—for him it is an imposed meaning. Yet
if one thinks of terminology, the shoe is on the other foot: Is the
meaning that a book has *before* it is placed in the Bible a biblical
meaning? Despite the meaning they have in themselves, the individual books of the Bible are not normative taken alone. (Indeed, a good
case can be made that any major book of the Bible taken by itself and
pressed to its logical conclusion will lead to heretical distortions.)
These books did not come down to us separately but as part of a collection,[15] and they were not accepted as authoritative by the Jewish
and Christian communities in isolation but as normative collection.
How then can one deny the designation "biblical meaning" to the
meaning they have as part of the Bible?

The real issue, with which I have more sympathy, is the relationship between the literal sense which a book has when it has left
the pen of the author (and/or redactor) and the canonical sense
which it has when seen in the context of its Testament or of the
whole Bible, especially when the change of meaning is substantial. In

---

[14]I am not certain with what theory of inspiration McEleney is working but the
theory advanced by Pope Leo XIII in *Providentissimus Deus,* which virtually presupposes a single author for a book, is not adequate to deal with many of the hermeneutic
problems that we face today—it does not cover the developmental process I have described above under a broader approach to the "literal sense." Moreover, respectable
Catholic scholars extend the inspiration/inerrancy discussion precisely to the canonical process, e.g., P. Benoit, "The Inspiration of the Septuagint," in *Jesus and the Gospel* (New York: Herder and Herder, 1973) 1–10; N. Lohfink, "The Inerrancy and the
Unity of Scripture," TD 13 (1965) 185–92.

[15]At times there were partial collections, e.g., the (five books of the) Law, or the
Prophets, or the Pauline Letters; and canons varied for groups within Judaism and for
churches of different regions.

part, this may be an issue treated in literary and philosophical studies; for in both fields it is often affirmed that a writing, once composed, has a life of its own, and so the literal sense of the author's intent cannot absolutely control meaning.[16] While I agree with that, I would still lend a preponderant importance to the literal sense in exegetical investigation.[17] Even when the quest of a larger sense has uncovered spiritual and theological possibilities that go beyond the literal sense and those possibilities have been accepted in Christian thought, the literal sense (which did not include those possibilities) remains a conscience and a control. Some use the word "criterion"; but that may imply that developments not justified by the literal sense are wrong,[18] and that is too absolute. It is rather a control toward which one must be responsible, even if responsibility is exercised by recognizing the inadequacy of the literal sense. Granted the difficulty of historical-critical research and the alien character of a book completed 2000 to 3000 years ago, there will always be an innate tendency to skip over lightly the quest for the literal sense—especially on the part of beginners and on the part of those whose primary interest is elsewhere (theologians, philosophers, literati). To

---

[16]See P. Ricoeur, *Interpretation Theory: Discourse and the Surplus of Meaning* (Fort Worth: Texas Univ., 1976); H.-G. Gadamer, *Truth and Method* (New York: Seabury, 1975). In American Catholic thought, Sandra M. Schneiders has sought to apply the principles of Ricoeur and Gadamer to the Bible.

[17]It is not clear to me to what extent those who emphasize "canonical context" or "canonical criticism" give preponderance to the meaning derived from historical criticism. Very interesting is the critique of B. S. Childs' views by J.A. Sanders, "Canonical Context and Canonical Criticism," *Horizons in Biblical Theology* 2 (1980) 173–97. In Sanders' view canonical criticism is a subdiscipline of biblical criticism; but what percentage of effort should be devoted to it as compared to another subdiscipline, historical criticism? I am not asking for an exact mathematical response, but an indication of where the various canonical critics stand on the issue. The same needs to be asked of those interested in the approach described in the previous footnote.

[18]A. Dulles, "Ecumenism and Theological Method," *Journal of Ecumenical Studies* 17 (1980–81) 40–48, esp. 43, criticizes H. Küng's attempt to make the criterion of all theology "the original Christian message itself... analyzed by historical critical analysis." I agree with this criticism if criterion is understood as described above (a norm to which all must conform), but such a message is *a* criterion in the sense of something which enters importantly into the evaluation of all Christian theology. One may never ignore the literal sense of Scripture, and Christians must be aware of and justify instances in which they seriously differ from it.

start off students with a preponderant emphasis on the canonical sense (or any other larger sense), or to begin theological discussions with the broader applicabilities of Scripture may be a wrong pedagogy. Although one must grant the legitimacy of the more-than-literal meaning, it is an essential discipline to struggle for the literal meaning, so that one may be aware of how far one has gone beyond it.

WHAT THE BIBLE MEANS

Many modern scholars would be content to stop with the canonical sense of Scripture, i.e., with the meaning that a book has as part of the biblical collection. B. S. Childs states (*Introduction*, 83): "A canonical Introduction is not the end, but only the beginning of exegesis." I would carry that statement farther by insisting that the canonical sense which the biblical books were seen to have when they were placed in the canon in a past century (the 4th century served much of Christianity as the terminus for the canon-forming process) marked only a stage in the unfolding of the meaning of the Bible. The very existence of the Bible understood as a normative collection of books supposes an ongoing community willing to shape itself by responding to that norm. Childs (*Introduction,* 80–82) would surely admit that, but he is not lucidly clear as to whether such an ongoing process is only a matter of "receiving and transmitting the authoritative Word" or is actually formative of biblical meaning. I would contend that the way in which the Church in its life, liturgy, and theology comes to understand the Bible[19] is constitutive of "biblical meaning," because it is chiefly in such a context that this collection is serving as the Bible for believers. We are not dealing merely in such an instance with application, accommodation, or eisegesis; we are

---

[19]This process has continued from the moment of canon formation until the present moment, and a thorough study of the hermeneutical issue would involve the interrelation of various stages of church interpretation, which are not always harmonious among themselves. Here I shall concentrate upon what a passage means to the contemporary Church; and even then I cannot deal with the problem that a passage may not mean the same thing in all sections of the Church, or even the same thing in liturgy and theology. Obviously I am approaching the question from a Christian viewpoint; a Jewish scholar might be concerned with what the Hebrew Scriptures came to mean in the rabbinic academies and the synagogues.

dealing with the issue of what a biblical book *means,* as distinct from what it *meant,* either when it was written (literal sense) or when it became part of the canonical collection (canonical sense[20]).

Having affirmed this, I would argue that we need to be precise on how "what it meant" and "what it means" can be related in Roman Catholicism, especially in light of the Vatican II principle enunciated above which gives "the task of authentically interpreting the word of God . . . to the living teaching office of the Church." The following observations are meant to aid that precision.

(1) *It is crucial that we be aware that the church interpretation of a passage and the literal sense of that passage may be quite different.* Let me give some practical examples of the way in which I have encountered the failure to understand that difference. Recently I reported on how different priesthoods are described in the Bible, a report that now constitutes Chapter Six below. D. J. Unger, a priest who in times past has written on the Bible, composed an indignant letter to the *Pittsburgh Catholic* Newspaper (May 2, 1980) complaining about the distinction I made between the priesthood of Jesus Christ described in Hebrews (the unique priesthood of the Divine Son) and the cultic priesthood associated with the eucharist by the Church of the second century as an heir to the Levitical priesthood of Israel—a priesthood not described in the NT. Unger wrote that the cultic priesthood is a "function of Christ's priesthood as the Popes have said repeatedly," and he urged the readers of the newspaper to ignore me and to read John Paul II's Holy Thursday message for the Catholic teaching about the priesthood. I accept the teaching of the popes as much as Father Unger does, but that teaching in no way shows what was in the mind of the author of Hebrews whose words about the uniqueness of Christ's priesthood and the once-for-

---

[20]Paradoxically, then, "canonical sense" does not mean for me the sense that is once and for all times normative. Those who wrote the biblical books and gave to them what we call the literal sense had a partial insight into truth; so did those who formed the canon and thus gave to the books their canonical sense; the Church has another partial insight when it finds a meaning for those books in its own life. The quest for meaning is open-ended, and the interaction of these various senses provides the excitement and wealth of exegesis. It is a challenge to do exegesis constructively and yet not blandly.

all character of his sacrifice would be very hard to understand if he thought there were Christian cultic priests and the eucharist was a sacrifice. In associating the Christian form of the Levitical priesthood with the priesthood according to the order of Melchizedek, the Church has clearly gone beyond the NT and, indeed, in a direction that might have made some of its authors unhappy. Knowing clearly the first-century situation need not lead one to deny the validity of subsequent development; but it makes intelligible why other Christians reject the notion of a Christian cultic priesthood, and it warns (as I indicate in Chapter Six) against allowing the cultic priesthood an exclusive domination in Roman Catholic thought about priesthood.

I can illustrate the failure to distinguish between church interpretation and the literal sense in another way. In my *Birth of the Messiah* (Garden City: Doubleday, 1977) 9, I wrote: "I see no reason why a Catholic's understanding of what Matthew and Luke meant in their infancy narratives should be different from a Protestant's." Manuel Miguens[21] asks, "Does Brown mean that Protestants are generally right and Catholics generally wrong?" (After seeing such exegesis of my statement, I can understand why those who have reviewed Miguens' books, as reported above, do not value highly the objectivity of his attempts to interpret Scripture.) My statement has no such deprecatory intent. What "Matthew and Luke meant" is the literal sense of their Gospels; and critical scholars, whether Catholic or Protestant, have to use the same methods in determining that sense. But perhaps what is behind such a polemical attitude toward my statement is better understood from the work of another writer who misinterprets me. J. T. O'Connor[22] cites my statement correctly but then goes on to refute it by changing its wording: "A Catholic's understanding of what Matthew and Luke *mean* in their infancy narratives cannot be the same as a Protestant's" to the extent that Catholic tradition informs the Catholic's understanding of the written word of God. I have italicized the present tense of the verb to

---

[21]*Communio* 7 (1980) 52.

[22]"Mary, Mother of God and Contemporary Challenges," *Marian Studies* 29 (1978) 26–43, specifically 36–37.

show how he has misrepresented my view.[23] Of course, it is precisely in the area of what the infancy narratives *mean* to the Christian community that I would expect a difference between Catholics and Protestants (e.g., in terms of mariology), but not in terms of what the infancy narratives meant to Matthew and Luke.

(2) *The role of church authority in interpreting the Bible has been more properly in the area of what Scripture means than in the area of what Scripture meant.* For me the principle that the teaching office of the Church can authentically interpret the Bible is more important now than ever before, granted the diversity and contrariety among biblical authors uncovered by historical criticism. Cardinal Baum[24] has spoken eloquently of the situation: "The 'evidence' of Scripture—both to the scholar and even to the believer . . . —is *of itself* inconclusive in determining the meaning of the most fundamental tenets of the Christian faith: the identity of Jesus, the meaning of his life and death, the nature of his triumph, the obligations imposed on his followers, the consequences of his life for us, etc." In that situation church guidance is supremely important, but it does *not* aid the cause of church authority if we inflate into unreality the area of its authority. We must be clear as to just where in the search for biblical meaning church authority plays its role.

Certainly it is unrealistic to expect the church to settle questions of biblical composition, authorship, dating, etc. Confusion has arisen on that score from the decrees of the Roman Pontifical Biblical Commission in the period 1905–1915 which gave precise directions on such questions, setting as Catholic policy the unicity of Isaiah, the apostolic authorship of Matthew and John, the genuinely Pauline character of Hebrews and the Pauline authorship of the Pastorals,

---

[23]It would please me if this misrepresentation was indeliberate. I note, however, that later O'Connor (p. 42) cites me as holding what he regards as a dangerous view, namely, that, were (contrary-to-fact) Joseph the human father of Jesus, this would not have excluded the fatherhood of God, which is an ontological not a biological concept. In so doing, O'Connor conveniently neglects to tell his readers how I emphasized that Cardinal Ratzinger, one of the most respected conservative theologians in Roman Catholicism, holds the same view (see VCBRJ 42); also TS 33 (1972) 16.

[24]*The Washington Star,* Sunday Jan. 27, 1980, section G.

Mary's responsibility for the *Magnificat,* etc. The Church was not simply taking a cautionary position, warning against the possible dangers of "new" views; it was invoking authority to bind scholars to internal obedience on such questions. Some may want to debate whether the Church can do that, but the history of the episode warns at least that the Church *should* not do that. Within less than 50 years the secretary of the same Pontifical Biblical Commission (JBC, art. 72, #25) found himself giving Catholics "full freedom" with regard to the previous decrees; and certainly today it would be hard to find a majority of Catholic scholars taking even one of the positions inculcated in 1905–1915. In Catholic belief the authorities of the Church are guided by the Holy Spirit in matters of faith and morals, but scarcely in matters of date and authorship; and so one may ask by what authority the Church could decide such issues. It is quite indefensible to claim that such issues are inextricably intertwined with matters of faith and morals, since no doctrine of the Church depends on who wrote a book and at what time, so long as one allows that the book is inspired. Nor is an appeal to tradition satisfactory, for in questions of authorship the church writers simply copied each other (or expanded what they received with legendary additions). Most of the time the "tradition" about such an issue, however unanimous, has little more value than the credibility of the first attestation.

Limitations also affect the ability of church authorities to settle questions of historical fact, very few of which are intrinsic to doctrine. Outside the general acceptance that Jesus lived and was crucified, the only facts of his career that have become part of specific doctrines seem to be that he was conceived without a human father, that his body did not corrupt in the grave, and that at a supper before he died he related bread and wine to his own flesh and blood. Other doctrines are scarcely pinned down to the historicity of a specific incident.[25] The Church has defined Mary's continued virginity in such a way that the "brothers" of Jesus mentioned in the NT can-

---

[25]The affirmation that in order for a particular doctrine to be true a particular fact must be historical needs to be proved in every case. Our history from Galileo on is filled with the wrong identification between doctrine and a customary, but not necessarily accurate, articulation of that doctrine in terms of historical facts.

not have been Mary's children (a position I accept as a Catholic) but by what authority can the Church tell us positively who they were? One may reply that there was a virtually unanimous tradition in the West that they were Jesus' cousins, based on Jerome's rejection of an earlier tradition that they were his stepbrothers as children of Joseph by a previous marriage. To my mind the existence of such a tradition in a matter that is not of faith and morals (i.e., the exact identity of the relatives) does not of itself establish truth. Did Jerome have special historical information on this question not available to others? Is Jerome's exegesis of the pertinent texts convincing? Is Jerome's theological interest in the virginity of Joseph compelling? Those are the questions that decide the validity of a tradition that cannot authenticate itself simply by being tradition. The necessity of caution about tradition is no hypothetical problem. On pp. 38f. of the article discussed above, J. T. O'Connor criticizes my exegesis of the infancy narratives: "Brown will not use the Catholic tradition as an objective element aiding his exegesis of the text." He assumes that there has "always" been a community tradition that family testimony supports the virginal conception. I would respond that the virginal conception is doctrine; the idea that a family testimony is our source of information is not doctrine, and any tradition to that effect must be judged not on the basis of the Holy Spirit guiding the Church but on the basis of the evidence that supports such a tradition. In point of fact there is no first-century claim to such testimony; it appears later in the apocryphal *Protevangelium of James,* thus named because it is supposed to be a work by a stepbrother of Jesus. The facts narrated by the *Protevangelium* are demonstrably fictitious. What really gave rise to the tradition that Joseph and Mary respectively were the sources of the infancy narratives of Matthew and Luke was the observation that Joseph was the main character in Matthew's story and Mary the main character in Luke's story. The fact that this tradition was accepted for centuries means nothing if its basis is shown by historical criticism to be implausible. The Church is the ultimate judge of faith and morals; historical criticism is the criterion of history— confused transfer in either direction can have disastrous results.

Limited too is the ability of church authorities to determine the literal sense of a passage of Scripture. In Scripture interpretation the reason for turning to church authority guided by the Holy Spirit is that such interpretation affects the way people believe and live. What a passage *means* to Christians is the issue for the Church—not the semi-historical issue of what it *meant* to the person who wrote it. We see this from the fact that normal Roman Catholic Church intervention into exegesis has been to *reject* an interpretation that represents an intolerable challenge to its life, e.g., the rejection of Reformation attempts to prove from Scripture that there should be only two or three sacraments. To the best of my knowledge the Roman Catholic Church has never defined the literal sense of a single passage of the Bible.[26]

It needs to be underlined that the use of Scripture in doctrinal statements composed by church authorities in a pre-critical period may *not* be read as the answer to historical-critical problems raised subsequently. It has been affirmed by the Roman Doctrinal Congregation[27] that doctrines enunciated by the magisterium solve only certain questions and are sometimes phrased in the changeable conceptions of a given epoch. That must be remembered when we relate such doctrines to modern biblical questions. Tridentine statements that Christ instituted seven sacraments (DBS 1601) and that by the words "Do this in commemoration of me" Christ ordained the apostles priests (DBS 1752) represent an interpretation of the general thrust of the whole NT for the life of the Church. They do not and will not answer historical-critical questions such as: Did the historical Jesus have a clear idea of sacrament? In his earthly life how many of what we call sacraments did he consciously envision? Before his death did Jesus actually utter the words "Do this in commemoration of me" (missing in Matthew's and Mark's account of the Last Supper), or is that a post-resurrectional interpretation of the implication of his Last Supper based upon the eucharistic practice of the primitive churches known to Luke (22:19) and Paul (I Cor 11:25)? Did the Jesus of the earthly ministry think of any of his followers as cultic priests and did he think of the eucharist as a sacrifice? These questions are best answered, not by citing church doctrine phrased by people who were neither asking nor answering

---

[26]See JBC art. 71, #87, which gives attention to what is sometimes (but dubiously) presented as an exception, i.e., Vatican I's use of Matt 16:17–19.

[27]For the pertinent passage of *Mysterium Ecclesiae* (1973) see BRCFC 116–18.

them, but by studying the Gospels historically and seeking to pierce behind the professions of early faith to the circumstances of Jesus' ministry and his world view. Even if many of them are answered in the negative, however, this does not mean that the subsequent Roman Catholic Church was wrong at Trent in insisting that its doctrines of seven sacraments, eucharistic sacrifice, and priestly ordination were a valid interpretation of Scripture—an interpretation of what by symbiosis Scripture had come to mean in church life, but not necessarily an interpretation of what it meant in the mind of those who wrote the pertinent passages.

(3) *Tension is not an improper relationship between what the Scripture meant to its authors and what it has come to mean in the Church.* Other theories would stress absolute harmony, or contradiction, or development that is always congruous; but there are difficulties in each of those suggestions. Obviously the literal sense of a biblical passage and the church usage of that passage will often be harmonious, but my point (1) above insists that the two senses can be different. Yet personally I would not accept the opposite extreme which allows the literal meaning and the church interpretation to be contradictory in the strict sense. If one takes an example from the few doctrines that I have mentioned above as including or presupposing specific historical facts, some would not be disturbed by a situation in which historical criticism would make it virtually certain that Jesus was conceived normally, even though church doctrine speaks of a virginal conception. Yet that is modernism in the classic sense whereby doctrines are pure symbols that do not need to be correlated at all with the facts of which they speak. On the other hand, just as problematic is the contention that an exegete who accepts the church doctrine of virginal conception must establish by critical investigation that Jesus had no human father. In fact, most often in such instances historical investigation will leave an ambiguity, so that church doctrine will be neither in clear harmony nor in sharp contradiction with the results, but will need its own theological basis.

A more sophisticated Catholic thesis would seek to trace a congruous development from the literal sense of Scripture to the church interpretation of Scripture (or church doctrine based on Scripture). Careful historical study, however, does not always support such a benevolent picture. The church position may follow directly from some trends in Scripture but not from others. For instance, the episcopal-presbyteral structure is a prolongation of the direction incipient in the Pauline Pastorals, but is quite alien to some Johannine sensitivities. A developed mariology lies on a trajectory that begins with Luke's picture of Mary as the first Christian but finds little support in the Marcan judgment that Mary did not understand Jesus. Granted a tension, then, between church positions and some strains of Scripture, is that tension harmful? Must it always be relativized by Catholics in absolute favor of the doctrine, so that the literal sense of the contrary biblical passage is explained (away) as a partial insight of an imperfect past? Joseph Ratzinger,[28] now a very influential cardinal, faulted Vatican II for stressing only the harmony of Scripture and tradition and not recognizing the critical use of one to adjudicate the other. If the tension I have described is seen as an opportunity rather than as a threat, its critical impact may be helpful in many ways to a Church that lives by tradition as well as by Scripture.

For instance, some church doctrines vocalize a theological insight in historical phraseology, and a knowledge of the biblical picture may help to distinguish what is really important in that combination. It is Catholic doctrine that the bishops have been placed by the Spirit as successors of the apostles (DBS 1768, 3061), and often that dogma has been identified with the thesis that the apostles themselves chose and ordained the bishops who in turn ordained their successors. As we shall see in Chapter Eight, this understanding finds its first attestation in Clement of Rome (42:4) at the end of the first century (but there without the claim that *all* bishops were appointed by apostles). It is challenged by a work of equal antiquity, the *Didache* (15:1), which tells a community that seemingly does not yet have such officials: "Appoint [ordain] for yourselves bishops and deacons." The NT gives evidence that apostles like Paul may have appointed bishops (or presbyters) in some of the churches, but no evidence that this was a common apostolic practice. One should not polemically relativize the silence and negative evidence in

---

[28]In *Commentary on the Documents of Vatican II*, ed. H. Vorgrimler (5 vols.; New York: Herder and Herder, 1969) 3. 193.

favor of succession through linear ordination; one should rather recognize that apostolic succession did not require linear, tactile ordination in the first centuries and that a later practice has been too
simply equated with the doctrine. That does not mean that the
Church cannot insist on linear episcopal ordination now, but it
makes intelligible why other Christians may not see the need of such
ordination and makes less unthinkable an occasional exception allowed to achieve Christian unity, were that advisable.

Besides clarifying doctrine, the tension between church interpretation and the meaning of Scripture discovered through historical
criticism may result in the modification of exaggerations. Positions
taken by the Church represent a partial grasp of truth and a choice
made at a price; and opposing voices from the Bible may help to preserve what would otherwise be lost. I have mentioned that Job and
Sirach denied an afterlife. To a Church that has opted for Jesus' positive attitude toward an afterlife the voice of Job still has something
important to say. Anticipation of an afterlife often leads people to neglect the importance of encountering God in this life—a neglect challenged by Job who could take God so seriously even though he
thought that there was only this life with all its misery.

*   *   *

I shall not prolong this chapter by examples of how this tension
can benefit the Church. Harmony between the Church's stance and
the views of the biblical authors helps to assure the Church of its
apostolic continuity; occasional lack of harmony can remind the
Church of the vicissitudes of history and of human limitations. The
literal sense of Scripture uncovered through historical-critical research may challenge the Church; it is incumbent on scholars to
present that challenge not hostilely but by way of invitation. The
challenge should not be feared or neutralized by the generalization
that the scholarship behind it is uncertain and never unanimous—
that has always been so, but that does not free the Church from the
obligation of using the best scholarship available. Scripture would
not be the word of God if it always confirmed Christians or the
Church, for the God who inspired the Scriptures is a God whose

thoughts are not our thoughts. Jesus is not heard if at times he is not reminding God's people that we are capable of transgressing the commandments of God for the sake of our own traditions (Matt 15:3). A Bible at times in tension with the Church can serve as the conscience of the Church reminding it that it is not yet what it should be.

Chapter Three
SCHOLARS AGAINST
THE CHURCH:
FACT OR FICTION?

Summary of the theme:[1] *Tensions between what a biblical author meant historically and what the Bible means to the Church today brings scholarship into dialogue with church authority. Many fictions surround this dialogue as if it were always a hostile confrontation. Debunking the fictions gives us a more accurate idea of the limits and strengths of each party in the tasks of discerning and proclaiming divine revelation.*

In the last chapter we saw the role of scholars and their historical-critical method in determining what the biblical authors *meant*. We saw also the pre-eminent role of the Church in determining what the Bible *means*. Thus both scholars and church teachers make a contribution toward determining the meaning of the Bible, and in subsequent chapters of this book I shall stress the cooperation that must exist between the two. Yet there is abroad in Roman Catholicism an impression that scholars and church authorities are locked in struggle; that the Church distrusts theologians, and that theolo-

---

[1]The material represented in this chapter was originally delivered at the 75th annual convention of the National Catholic Educational Association at St. Louis, Mo., on March 29, 1978, under the title: "The Magisterium Vs. the Theologians—Debunking Some Fictions." It was published in *Origins* 7 (#43, April 13, 1978) 673–82; and in CM 76 (Sept. 1978) 13–29.

gians despise bishops. Much of this struggle is pure fiction; but it is worth a chapter to debunk such a view lest my hope for cooperation seem a dream.

SOME GENERAL OBSERVATIONS

Let me begin by defining my terms. For brevity I shall use "theologians" to cover biblical scholars, systematic or dogmatic theologians, ethicists, and church historians—all those who contribute to the scientific study of God's revelation. And I shall use "magisterium" for the pope and the bishops (in council or out), even though I am aware that this usage is relatively recent, and that some theologians contest such an exclusive usage on the grounds that it does not do justice to the previously more active role of the *magister theologiae* (the medieval teacher of theology). Be that as it may, I tend to be pragmatic about terminology. Many of my biblical confreres use the term "myth" in relation to the NT, arguing eloquently and correctly that it need not connote falsehood. But since it has a connotation of falsehood for most people, I avoid the term in my study of the NT simply because I think it raises more difficulty than it is worth, and that a circumlocution which does not cause resentment serves more effectively to communicate the nuance I desire. Similarly "magisterium" is a fighting word; I think the attempt to reclaim it for theologians will not succeed; and I personally do not think the battle worth fighting so long as, under any other name, the legitimate role of theologians in shaping the teaching of the Church is respected.

In estimating that role I recognize that I may be more modest than some of my Catholic theologian friends. All that I want is that scholarly evidence be taken into account in the formulation or reformulation of Catholic doctrine and that theologians be sincerely treated as dialogue partners to be listened to (not obeyed). If I may be permitted to quote myself to show that I have remained very consistent on this point, in dealing with the sensitive topics of the virginal conception and bodily resurrection (VCBRJ 12), I stated:

> A responsible answer to these questions must take into account the evidence as scholars view it today. Notice that

what I ask is that the answer *take into account* the scholarly evidence. It would be sheer nonsense for me to pretend
that scholars can give the Catholic answer to these questions. When it is a question of doctrinal teaching, it is the
Church through its various organs of teaching and belief
that gives the answer. Thus I offer here no ammunition for
the charge that theological scholars are usurping the rights
of the magisterium of the Church by their investigations of
past doctrines with an eye to possible modification. For the
most part theologians are quite aware that the evidence
they offer must be assessed within the wider context of the
Church's life guided by the Spirit and are only too happy to
put their evidence at the service of the magisterium.

If that past statement of mine may seem to some theologians not
to do justice to their understanding of the role they should have, I
am sure that to some on the other side it will seem too slighting of
their understanding of the magisterium. After all, I said that *the
Church* gives the answer "through its various organs of teaching and
belief"; I did not say that the magisterium alone gives the answers.

Perhaps both the magisterium and theologians need to be more
sensitive in making claims to authority, lest we give to the Church
and the world the impression that we have confused the priorities of
our Master. He criticized the heathen rulers for exercising authority
over people and ordered: "It shall not be so among you" (Mark
10:42–43). His statement does not negate the need for authority, but
it warns us against making the struggle for authority a priority.

In discussing the question of teaching authority, there are two
abuses to which we should be alert. The first is too simple an assignment of responsibilities; the second is too simple an understanding of
the way in which one exercises the responsibility one has. A good example of a simplistic assignment of responsibilities is the unqualified
equation of the pope and bishops with the *ecclesia docens* ("teaching
Church") and theologians and everyone else with the *ecclesia discens*
("learning Church"). At one time or another and in some way, everyone in the Church is part of the *ecclesia docens*—and indeed, very
visibly, the women and men (the order of the sexes is deliberate) to
whom parishes and schools have entrusted the formal religious edu-

cation of the next generation. And, at one time or another and in some way, everyone in the Church is also part of the *ecclesia discens,* including pope and bishops. Again the words of our Master are almost a reproach: "You have only one Teacher—all the rest of you are brothers [and sisters]" (Matt 23:8).

Once we have recognized that the responsibilities of teaching and learning are assigned in different ways to all, we must not exercise those responsibilities in independence of each other but by cooperation. I have said above that theologians must put their evidence at the service of the magisterium and not pretend to give *the* Catholic answer to disputed points. Similarly the magisterium must draw upon theologians in making its contribution to the Church's answer. In PB 76-77 I told a story that has been cited again and again in the ultraconservative press as an example of arrogance, whereas I think it is a basic lesson about what should be in the Church. I mentioned that a bishop, now deceased, was welcoming several biblical scholars into his diocese, and that he remarked that his own Scripture course in the seminary had been hopeless and consequently he never felt confident about even the exegesis of Scripture needed for preaching. Yet at the same time he cautioned the scholars that only the bishops could speak authoritatively about Scripture! And I remarked: "Here was a man innocently claiming that he could speak authoritatively about a subject in which, as he had just admitted, he had not even elementary competence."

I would still make that remark: I do not think that the members of the magisterium can speak authoritatively about matters of theology or Scripture unless they have elementary competence in the field, either by their own learning or by consultation. I recognize fully that the office of pope and bishop is a charism that involves divine help; but, as far as I know, in good Catholic theology grace is thought to cooperate with nature. To use properly the teaching role that is theirs by the charism of their office, bishops must take the step of learning about what they are teaching—that is not only common sense; it is the age-old understanding of the Church. Ah, the charge will come back, you are saying that bishops must listen to the theologians and thus become their mouthpieces. No, I am saying that bishops must listen to theologians and acquire information, and pray over it, and think over it, and then teach pastorally what they judge the Church must hear. But, as part of the *ecclesia discens* and *docens,* the first step of any Catholic is to listen and to learn.

I have made these general remarks about the magisterium and theologians and how I understand their roles simply that my own position may be clear. I have not the slightest intention of lecturing members of the hierarchy or my fellow theologians on their responsibilities. As will become clear, I think they both know their responsibilities and are exercising them well. My fear is that third parties do not always understand well the roles of bishops and of theologians and that some wish to increase division rather than to increase cooperation, which is my goal. But before I turn to the heart of this chapter which is directed toward lessening the scope of division, let me make one more general observation to place my theme in focus. Division between the magisterium and theologians is not the number one problem or even the number two problem that faces the Church in the world or in the United States. One might give higher rank to the problem if it were phrased more broadly: "How does the Church teach with authority in these times?" But that would mean a recognition that there are more alternatives in the answer than "Listen to the magisterium" or "Listen to the theologians."

In NT times the man who wanted to know "What must I do to inherit eternal life?" did not go to the priests and the scribes (the Jewish equivalent of magisterium plus theologians); he went to the "Good Teacher" whose own life gave visible indication that he knew something about eternal life (Mark 10:17). Today Mother Teresa of Calcutta can command a larger audience than either bishop or theologian when she talks about what it means to be a Christian. Saints teach authoritatively, and with a different kind of authority than either the magisterium or theologians. But even then we have not exhausted the alternatives, and the question of who teaches our Catholic people with authority is not always solved so positively. In fact, Catholics give tremendous authority to what they hear about religion on the media and to what other people are doing in matters of morals and religious observance. The real significance of the question whether to listen to the magisterium or to the theologians may lie in the somewhat desperate hope that in making decisions Catholics get some "input" of substance whether by way of tradition or by way of responsible modern theology, and do not settle for gleanings from "pop" presentations. Neither papal encyclical, nor bishops' pastoral, nor theological tractate has the direct religious impact on many American Catholics of an article in the religion section of *Time* and *Newsweek,* or of a half hour prime-time treatment on national television. That realization not only relativizes the importance of the dispute between the magisterium and theologians; it makes such a dispute more tragic.

FOUR FICTIONS

Yet I wish to sound a hopeful note in this chapter, for I think the dispute between theologians and the magisterium has been greatly exaggerated. This dispute is surrounded with fiction; and true to my vocation as a biblical scholar I would like to "demythologize" some of the fiction, if just this once I may cede to the frequent misuse of the term "demythologize."[2] In instances when the magisterium and theologians disagree, people must learn to diagnose correctly such disagreement. I wish to point out four fictions involved in the popular Catholic presentation of the disagreement so that people may be able to deal intelligently with the relatively few instances where there is real disagreement.

First Fiction: *In matters of Catholic doctrine the main opponents are the magisterium (pope and bishops) and theologians.*

In fact, third parties are much more frequently in public disagreement with both the magisterium and the main body of Catholic theologians over doctrine than those two groups are in disagreement with each other. By "third parties" I think particularly of how the communications media have been employed by groups who stand at opposite ends of the religious spectrum. On the one hand, there is a religious view that finds vocalization in the national television and the great secular newspapers which is quite critical of the Roman Catholic position on matters of morals and religious education. On the other hand, the ultraconservative bloc of Catholic newspapers

---

[2]It is often used, as I misuse it here, to describe the removal of mythology from a narrative in order to reach historical fact. It really means to reinterpret the ancient mythological expressions into modern terms, so that the point of the narrative may be more easily grasped.

and magazines is quite critical of what they regard as the dissolution of traditional Catholicism. Both these critiques are much more acerbic than the critique of bishops by the theologians or vice versa. It is rare that you find a major theologian whose disagreement with the magisterium is not respectful; and it is increasingly rare for an American bishop to indulge in the "so-called theologians" calumny when he is disagreeing with theologians of note. I find that third parties are much less careful when they go after either theologians or bishops. Let me give some examples.

The liberal elements in the secular media do not indulge in invective against church authorities (as sometimes do the liberal elements in the Catholic media). But when the pope or bishops issue any statement contrary to the "with-it" trends of our times, especially in questions of sexual morals, there is thinly veiled contempt in the reporting. One way or another the audience is reminded that those who composed the statement are older celibates, religious leaders who do not have their feet on the ground and who are hewing to the party line. To show that these leaders are out of touch with the Catholic laity, there is usually brought forward to comment on the statement a representative of a more contemporary Catholicism (a nun, a priest, or a lay person) who inevitably begins: "While I respect the position in the statement, I do not believe that this is where most Catholics are." What else can the audience conclude but that those who composed the church statement are "out of it." The liberal third party rarely extends the attack to modern Catholic theologians because of a belief (or a wish to create the illusion) that most Catholic theologians reject the church statements as well. In fact, liberals are often genuinely nonplussed when they consult a Catholic theologian of note on such a matter and do not get a liberal answer. You can almost hear the silent surprise: "You are supposed to be on our side."

On the other side, the ultraconservative Catholic press is much less subtle in its assaults on both magisterium and theologians. The savage invective heaped upon Catholic theologians and biblical scholars in this press is well known: "so-called priests, Modernists, crypto-Protestants, Judases, latter day Herods, subverters of the faith." More startling is the extension of this invective to the bishops. "Bishops in the dark" screams a headline on an article which charges that bishops are now the enthusiastic backers of the great rebellion against Catholic belief. High members of the Church are said to be in active collaboration with the Communists; a cardinal is vilified as perhaps the greatest heretic the American Catholic Church has ever known; highly respected archbishops and bishops are denounced as undermining the faith of their people when they extend sponsorship to scholars disapproved of by the right; the Roman Pontifical Biblical Commission is described as having been taken over by Modernists; and American dioceses are charged with being in schism from Rome over the first confession/first communion issue. With increasing frequency the patronage of St. Thomas More is invoked: the gallant layman who stayed on the side of the pope when almost all the bishops of England betrayed the faith; and, of course, the ultraconservatives think they are doing just that in face of the betrayal of the faith by the bishops of our time. (Alas St. Thomas, most subtle author of *Utopia,* to have survived the barbarism of an arrogant king only to be lionized by the unnuanced of a later age—the latter fate may be worse than the first.) If this ultraconservative press does not go all the way (as did Archbishop Lefebvre) and attack the pope when they disagree with him, it is because they can present him as deceived by his liberal advisors, not knowing the iniquities of the American situation where the Church is increasingly passing into the hands of a Modernist hierarchy.

Of the two attacks on the magisterium and on theologians, challenging what they teach, the attack from the right may be noisier; but it speaks only to those already convinced and has no major effect on the thinking of American Catholics, especially now that death and age are removing from the scene the very few supporters that ultraconservatives have had in the hierarchy. The liberal contempt for church positions, particularly moral positions, is far more serious; and I think it does more to undermine the authority of the magisterium than does disagreement with theologians. (Some may object that the theologians are on the side of the secular liberals on moral matters; but that is calumny—the position of responsible Catholic moral theologians, even when they disagree with the bishops, is far more nuanced than the permissiveness encouraged in secular liberalism.) It is not my intent in this chapter to discuss how the magisterium and theologians should deal with attacks from the right and left. I simply wish to emphasize that the claim that Catholic doctrine is imperiled because of quarrels between the bishops and theologians is too simple. There is the massive presence of those who would constitute a "third magisterium" and would vie for authority in teaching with both bishops and theologians.

Leaving aside now third parties, let me explore some of the fiction about the extent of disagreement between the two recognized parties.

Second Fiction: *The prevailing relationship between the magisterium and Catholic theologians is one of disagreement.*

At times a significant group of noted Catholic theologians has expressed dissent from official statements of the pope or of the bishops, especially in matters of sexual morals. But the amount and frequency of this disagreement are seriously exaggerated in the mind of many Catholics, and I see at least two obvious reasons for this.

The first is the general negative thrust of "news." The air flight that crashes makes the headlines; the thousand flights that arrive safely are never mentioned. The general agreement of scholars with the positions of their Church, inherent in the very fact that they are practicing Roman Catholics, is not news; the occasional dissent is. A theologian or biblical scholar can give conferences in dioceses all over the country and be enthusiastically thanked by the respective bishops for contributing to the welfare of the Church; his lectures will be mentioned only in the local diocesan newspaper as part of the promotion. But let one bishop attack that scholar, and the item is on the NC News Service for distribution to every Catholic newspaper in the country. A book by a Catholic theologian on a sensitive subject may be distributed by 30 cardinals and bishops to every priest in their dioceses with the encouragement to read it; that is not a news item. The newspapers report only when a member of the hierarchy condemns a book.

The second factor that leads to an overstatement of disagreement is less inevitable and less innocent. Precisely because there are third parties who find the bishops too conservative or both the bishops and theologians too liberal, these third parties will tend to underline any sign of disagreement between bishops and theologians and exploit that disagreement to accomplish their own goal. Let me concentrate for a moment on a spate of recent actions that does just this. In recent years ultraconservative groups are making a big splash about founding *orthodox* Catholic colleges and *orthodox* catechetical institutes. The right to educate is *not* the issue of my concern here—I cede that gladly—but their action is deliberately phrased so as to cast doubt on the orthodoxy of recognized theologians teaching at the main Catholic centers of learning. The stress that a new college or institute is orthodox is a broad hint that all others are not. Ultraconservatives plead for the restoration of the Index of Forbidden Books and do not hesitate to reprimand bishops for giving *imprimaturs* to books which in their judgment belong on the Index. Such pleas and charges are meant to make Catholics think that very dangerous theologians are at work undermining the faith, when, in fact, those who are doing the protesting are often an alienated pressure group, so little open to change that their own orthodoxy may be questionable. The same process is at work on the liberal side when the bishops are mocked as being clearly out of step with *modern* Catholic thought. Half the time when I read what newspapers characterize as "modern Catholic thought," my first reaction is, "Deliver us from evil." It is often a mélange of superficial nonsense to which no serious theologian in my ken would lend support. And again such nonsense is being manipulated to portray a disagreement between the magisterium and theologians.

There is one example that I want to concentrate on and expose as a deliberate attempt to inflate the disagreement between the magisterium and theologians. We have been treated lately to a flurry of writing on the theme that the bishops are too soft on theologians, that they are not acting with sufficient decisiveness to wipe out dissent on matters of doctrine, that they should crack down since a large percentage of Catholic theologians are in open rebellion against the magisterium. In a way these complaints are an eloquent proof that the bishops do *not* see disagreement with theologians to be such a great problem—certainly not as great as militant vigilantes would make it. But as I look at such articles and note the names of the American theological scholars that the authors want condemned, the situation becomes even more paradoxical—many on the list are openly appreciated by the magisterium both here and abroad. In other words, the article entitled "Why Don't the Bishops Get Tough with the Theologians?" should really be titled "Why Are the American Bishops Listening to the Theologians Whom My Group Wants to Condemn?" Do not take my word for this; rather join me in a little, informal poll that I have been conducting on the side and test my results. Ask knowledgeable people (bishops, religious educators, editors of diocesan newspapers, teachers of theology) this question: "Who are the 10 most prominent Catholic theologians, moralists, and biblical scholars in the United States?"—not whether you like them or disagree with them—just the 10 most prominent American Catholic scholars in these fields. Making allowances for different choices, I have come up with about 15 names that appear on most lists. And I judge that 75 percent of the 15 named are very acceptable to the American bishops, as judged by their meeting at least several of the following criteria: their books are recommended by bishops to the priests or people; they are frequently invited to dioceses under the auspices of bishops; they are appointed to commissions set up under episcopal supervision; their books regularly appear with church approval. And I think this percentage is rather representative of the real relations between the magisterium and theologians in this country—75 percent or higher agreement. And so I contend that agreement and cooperation in the task of Catholic teaching is the prevailing picture between bishops and theologians, not disagreement. The citations I have given on the dedicatory page of this volume show that.

Third Fiction: *Theologians and magisterium can be spoken of as if they were monolithic groups, all of whom see doctrinal issues the same way.*

It is not an infrequent occurrence to see headlines like these: "Theologians deny papal infallibility"; "Biblical scholars deny the bodily resurrection"; "Catholic moralists disagree with Rome on homosexuality"; "Canonists say divorce is OK." The first reaction to those headlines should be to ask: "Which Catholic theologians? Which Catholic scholars?" Theologians and biblical scholars and canonists are not a monolithic group. I do not mean to emphasize the obvious that there are extremely liberal and extremely conservative theologians who disagree with the larger number of centrist theologians; I mean that even the centrists and moderate progressives are not a bloc. We all know of a Swiss Catholic theologian who denies infallibility; I can think of an American Catholic biblical scholar who denies the bodily resurrection of Jesus and of another biblical scholar who denies the virginal conception; I can think of an American Catholic moralist who thinks that homosexuality can be an acceptable and moral lifestyle. But I can think of many, many reputable and famous centrist Catholic theologians and biblical scholars who disagree firmly with such positions and have written against them.

I take for granted that the chief task of theologians and biblical scholars is to use the tools of their trade to seek meaning and truth. As Roman Catholics, they conduct their search for truth within the general framework of the traditional teachings of the Church and with loyalty to that tradition. But they are not primarily defenders of past positions. And so I am not surprised that in the course of seeking truth, they have to ask new questions, and to wonder whether old questions were properly heard when they were asked, and whether past responses really meet the nuances of modern problems. In asking such questions, one or the other theologian and biblical scholar may well emerge with a view startlingly different from the one that has been traditional in Catholicism. I am not surprised that those who have the primary pastoral responsibility for the faithful, the pope and bishops, may not wish that such a startlingly different view be disseminated from the pulpit or on the more elementary levels of religious training. But that is not necessarily a dispute between the magisterium and theologians. A more sensitive scholar will *not* wish his views to be disseminated on such a popular level until they have been discussed and honed by critique. And inevitably there will be other theologians of equal competence and adventurousness who will be harsher than the bishops in their critique of the startlingly different view, not on the grounds that the view is dangerous, but because they judge it implausible by the rules of theological and biblical methodology.

If the centrist bloc of theologians is far from univocal, neither is the magisterium, although differences in the confraternity of the pope and the bishops are expressed much more discreetly than differences among theologians. To the perceptive, it is clear that the majority of American bishops are not in complete agreement with certain Roman pastoral stances on the sacraments. Those who have sat in on the national meetings of the American bishops are impressed by the sharp differences of views expressed within that hierarchy. And when there have been votes on highly publicized issues, like communion-in-the-hand, it becomes clear that one bishop may regard an action as healthy for the Church, while another may regard it as a dangerous innovation. This should be remembered when a single bishop speaks out against theologians. It is perfectly possible, for instance, to have an ultraconservative member of the hierarchy align himself with right-wing forces and become their spokesman, condemning virtually every theologian in sight. This is not the magisterium vs. theologians; it is an extremist archbishop or bishop against theologians. It may be a mark both of sanity and of complete loyalty to present trends in the Church to have the disapproval of such a figure. His fellow bishops may judge his position to be hopelessly exaggerated, even if they do not express their feelings as publicly as do theologians about an exaggerated member of their guild. Among themselves bishops are properly wary of the maverick hierarch who is being lionized either by conservatives or by liberals as the ideal spokesman of the hierarchy—that designation usually means a spokesman for what a particular group of Catholics would like to have all bishops say.

Perhaps it would be in order to make a passing remark about the bishop who wishes to write and speak as a theologian in his own right—a theologian left, right, or center—rather than as a member of the hierarchy speaking for the Church. That must be made very clear, for the tendency otherwise will be to give the bishop's remarks more value than they have in themselves because of his position. If one wishes for the role of theologian, one must meet the same standards as other theologians. The standard questions must be asked about the bishop-theologian: Was he ever trained beyond the seminary level in theology or biblical studies; does he know the scientific literature; does he control the languages; and above all is he willing to submit an article, for example, to a magazine that has an editorial board which tests quality, like the *Catholic Biblical Quarterly* or *Theological Studies.* One becomes immediately suspicious when a bishop's articles consistently appear in a journal or newspaper that is an organ of propaganda for the extreme right and that is obviously delighted to use his name to support an already established conservative position. Finally, the bishop-theologian must be willing to have his views handled as roughly by theologians as they would handle those of a non-bishop.

Returning to the main issue, I would judge that a real controversy exists between the magisterium and theologians only when the pope or a whole group of bishops takes a stand opposed by a good number of theologians. The struggle between the majority on one side and the odd man out on the other is more a problem of eccentricity than of theology. But, since eccentricity can be exploited in these times by those who want to inflate the issue of disagreement, perhaps both theologians and bishops need more firmly to dissociate themselves from their respective eccentrics.

It may be objected that my comparison of diversity within the guild of theologians and diversity within the confraternity of bishops was not exact. I mentioned that theologians disagree with each other over things like the bodily resurrection, the virginal conception, the morality of homosexual behavior—in short, matters of faith and morals. Do bishops, representing the magisterium, disagree with each other on matters of church doctrine? To some extent the answer to that question depends on what one considers church doctrine, and this leads to a fourth fiction.

Fourth Fiction: *Theologians and the magisterium are in conflict because even centrist Catholic theologians deny many matters of church doctrine.*

Catholics are in a strange state of schizophrenia about church pronouncements. Those who inhabit the extreme right of the Catholic spectrum are eager to burn at the stake any theologian who disagrees with church pronouncements on sexual morality; but the necessity of accepting church positions becomes very vague if the bishops suggest returning the canal to Panama or come out in support of the farmworkers, or if Rome comes to an agreement with an Iron Curtain country. For this group, obedience is required in matters of faith and morals—and "morals" means sexual morals—but not in matters of social and political justice. On the other side of the spectrum, Catholic liberals taunt conservatives with non-observance of the social encyclicals, but preserve a glacial silence when the pope or the bishops speak about sexual morality. For them, bishops should be listened to if they say something progressive; but when they repeat tradition, that is just the party line. A reference to infallibility in faith and morals is looked on as archaic. Thus *selectivity toward church pronouncements has become a high art on all sides,* and that should be kept in mind when theologians are said to disobey church teachings. But I do not wish to excuse the disobedience of theologians on the grounds that "everyone is doing it." I wish rather to examine to what extent major theologians really do contradict Catholic doctrine. This can be answered only if one comes to grips, first, with inflated ideas about what constitutes Catholic doctrine, and second, with the realization that doctrines change.

First, an inflated and inexact idea about what constitutes Catholic doctrine. We have not erased from the general Catholic psyche the view that everything people were taught in catechism was Catholic doctrine. Half the bitter struggle over communion-in-the-hand and communion-under-two-species reflects the fact that people were taught that only the consecrated fingers of the priest should touch the sacred species or the chalice. Those who got a more refined education learned to distinguish such a pious custom (of dubious theological basis) from doctrine, but most people did not. Naturally, then, if theologians challenge such pious customs, they are thought to be opposing Catholic doctrine. I have noticed over and over again in the Catholic press instances where the reader would think that theologians were undermining Catholic doctrine but which did not involve matters of doctrine at all. For instance, a conservative group demands that a European theologian be censured for suggesting that the pope have a limited term of office and that his election be conducted by a more representative group than the College of Cardinals. The demand for censuring surely implies a grave deviation, does it not? Yet a Catholic is perfectly free to hold any view he or she wants about papal terms and elections, and I know that one of the most distinguished cardinals of the church shares on this point the views of the theologian in question.

Another example: a liberal reporter noted that in 1978 when the Epiphany was no longer a holy day of obligation in Italy, Pope Paul VI made a strong statement on the historicity of the Epiphany. (I doubt if any centrist theologian would question that, since epiphany means the manifestation of the Son of God in human form, which is certainly the most basic historical claim of Christianity.) Yet the reporter went on to speculate that the pope was implicitly criticizing biblical scholars who denied the historicity of the magi. Such gratuitous speculation creates theological confusion on many scores. The pope never mentioned the historicity of the magi. I know of no great number of Catholic biblical scholars who are denying the historicity of the magi. Of course, I do know that most Catholic scholars recognize that Matthew 2:1–12 is not a historical narrative in the way that the accounts of Jesus' ministry are historical; but it would go beyond the limitations of biblical method and beyond proof to say absolutely: "There were no magi." And finally, I have too much respect for Pope Paul VI to think that he would have so stretched the credibility of his office as to state solemnly that there were magi. The last several popes have been very discreet in not overcommitting themselves beyond questions of faith and morals, and most certainly the existence of the magi is not a matter of doctrine.

Still one more example of inflation of doctrine, this time on the conservative side. An editorial laments the evil fruit of recent biblical scholarship which has turned Catholics away from accepting the Scriptures and the Gospel as factual history. Certainly this is a sign of rebellion, is it not? Just the contrary—it is a sign of obedience, for the official teaching of the Catholic Church requires Catholics to hold that the Gospels are *not* literal accounts of the ministry of Jesus.[3] It is the editorial writer who is out of step with the Church's teaching.

I could go on and on, for the inflation of Catholic doctrine is often tendentious and deliberate on the part of those who wish to discredit centrist theologians. Statements of the Biblical Commission and of the Holy Office of the 1905–1920 anti-Modernist period are repeated over and over again as if they were Catholic doctrine, even though church authorities have explicitly granted freedom with re-

---

[3]"The truth of the story is not at all affected by the fact that the evangelists relate the words and deeds of the Lord in a different order, and express his sayings not literally but differently." *Instruction of the Pontifical Biblical Commission on the Historical Truth of the Gospels* (1964), Section IX. See BRCFC 111–15.

gard to many of these[4] and others have passed into desuetude.[5] The statements in the *Syllabus* of Pius IX are quoted as if they all had the same value as binding Catholic teaching, even though the most authoritative collection of church documents warns specifically against doing that (DBS p. 576). Such crass misuse of doctrine fed to ordinary Catholics will inevitably confuse them about the loyalty of responsible theologians who seek to work within the freedom that the Church gives them.

Second, what constitutes Catholic doctrine is obscured if one does not recognize change in doctrine. There are explicit statements of the Doctrinal Congregation (Holy Office) in *Mysterium Ecclesiae* (reported in BRCFC 116–18) about the historical conditioning of past church pronouncements. This is the Church itself coming to grips with what centrist theologians have been insisting on for years: All church dogma and doctrine have been phrased by human beings (with divine guidance to be sure), and thus doctrine is conditioned by the limitations of those who did the phrasing. The Holy Office declaration lists a series of limitations flowing from the expressive power of the language in use at a given time, from the fact that certain truths are expressed only partially, and that dogmas were meant to solve only certain questions, and were expressed in the changeable conceptions of a given epoch. Yes, it is the Doctrinal Congregation, not some wild-eyed theologian, that has taught solemnly and bindingly that the formulas of the past will not always be suitable for communicating the truth involved in them and that, with church approval, they may need to give way to new formulations. When it is claimed that some theologian is denying a past doctrine of the magisterium, one must remember this principle of the conditioned value of past formulas. One must ask whether the theologian is really denying the truth affirmed in that formula (which would bring him into true

---

[4]For the freedom granted by the secretary of the Pontifical Biblical Commission regarding decrees issued earlier in the century, see the 1955 statement quoted in BRCFC 110–11.

[5]For the basis of modifying the 1918 Holy Office statement on the human knowledge of Jesus by means of the responses to the Holy Office questionnaire of 1966, see JGM 41, n. 6; also Chapter Five below, n. 8.

conflict with the magisterium) or whether he is simply seeking a new formulation to meet a new problem not settled in the past (which is an investigation quite tolerable within the bonds of loyalty to the magisterium).

In summary, an intelligent understanding of the limits of Catholic doctrine, within guidelines given by the magisterium itself, means that very few modern theological investigations can be said to deny Catholic doctrine. In the fields of christology and ecclesiology Rome has expressed its public concern about only a few named European theologians and, in fact, has never officially labeled any one of them as guilty of heresy. In this country the disputes between the body of bishops and any large number of theologians have been in the field of ethics. If the bishops have handled these disputes gingerly,[6] it is not because they are weak or indecisive; but rather because, like many of us, they are beginning to appreciate more fully the complexities of truth and the way in which it is revealed, preserved and discovered— an appreciation singularly lacking in some who despise the bishops for not crushing the theologians, presumably on the principle that the first and greatest of all the commandments is "Hate one another for the love of God."

*   *   *

I have now finished my four fictions and hope that I have reduced to a more manageable size the relatively few times in which there is a direct conflict between the magisterium (pope and bishops) and a large number of representative Catholic theologians on matters of Catholic doctrine. If one can get rid of all the inflation, misunderstood or deliberate, we are not in such bad shape theologically. There are pains, but I suspect they are growing pains, not the pains of the expiring. Nevertheless, I have sympathy for those who are upset that even on a few issues there can exist serious disagreements between the magisterium and theologians. I wish I could share with them a

---

[6]The bishops (and Rome as well) have expressed clear disapproval of the *Human Sexuality* study which was "received" by the American Catholic Theological Society; but they have not been nearly severe enough to satisfy those who want the book condemned and its authors dismissed from teaching.

knowledge of church history so that they could realize that moments of disagreement within the Church are far from infrequent, and we are not the first generation of Catholics to face this dilemma. Indeed, I would judge that the NT Church had far more factions within it than has twentieth-century Catholicism.

And for those today who think that surely the end must be at hand because there are divisions,[7] know that there was a NT author who thought the same (I John 2:18). Frustrated by the presence of teachers whom he thought were wrong but who would not listen to him, he tried to give a principle of guidance to people who were confused by hearing contradictory teachings from the author and from his opponents. The principle he gave is *not* adequate to solve all church teaching problems for a long period of time, but it remains of help to those who think it a desperate problem that there are different teachers in the Church. The author of I John 2:27 wrote these words to those whom he called his little children: "As for you, the anointing received from Christ abides in your hearts; and so you have no need for anyone to teach you. Rather, inasmuch as his anointing teaches you about all things, it is true and free from any lie. And just as it taught you, so must you abide in him." In moments of confusion because of different teachers it is consoling to know that the Paraclete is given to everyone who loves Jesus and keeps his commandments (John 14:15–16) and that this Spirit of Truth does not leave us without guidance along the way of all truth (16:13).

---

[7] I shall indicate in Chapter Five below that, in my judgment, diversity (not division) in understanding a doctrine that is common to both sides can be enormously enriching to the Church.

Chapter Four
WHY DOES BIBLICAL SCHOLARSHIP MOVE THE CHURCH SO SLOWLY?

Summary of the theme:[1] *The New Testament affects many issues being debated among Christians and in the Church and so offers a particularly sensitive area for dialogue between scholars and church authorities. Hindrances have slowed each side in the dialogue, and these need to be recognized and overcome if biblical studies are to move the Church.*

The preceding chapter contended that disputes between theologians and biblical scholars, on the one side, and pope and bishops on the other are not nearly so frequent or serious as many would have us believe. Nevertheless, there remains an indisputable fact: positive cooperation between these two groups has been only partially achieved and moderately fruitful. I have been arguing in this book that modern biblical scholarship is of critical importance for Christians and the Church. Why are those implications so slowly grasped?

---

[1]The material represented in this chapter was originally delivered on the occasion of my being granted an honorary doctorate in Sacred Theology by the Catholic University of Louvain (June 30, 1976), as a gesture of recognizing American theology during the bicentennial year. It was published under the title "Difficulties in Using the New Testament in American Catholic Discussions" in *Louvain Studies* 6 (1976) 144–58, and in CM 75 (June 1977) 10–23.

What are the obstacles that prevent scholars and the magisterium from working together to move the Church? Let me illustrate how I would answer by discussing one field, namely, contemporary NT scholarship, and showing why I think it has been slow in affecting open and well-meaning members of the hierarchy, clergy, and laity. (Some years ago in BRCFC 3–19 I dealt with obstacles posed by ultra-conservatives whose outlook is hostile to modern centrist Catholic thought, but that is not my concern here.) I shall avoid the obvious and easy answer that some of these dialogue partners have never been exposed to the conclusions of critical NT investigations, for it would still be true that many who have read basic modern books by Catholic NT scholars have not seen the implications of this scholarship. Rather let me search for the answer in the quality of Catholic NT criticism and in the way it has been applied to problems facing Christians and the Church. My remarks flow from experience on the American scene, but most of what I say will be true of the larger English-speaking world as well.

By way of anticipation, let me state the two theses that I shall offer as partial answers and that will serve as the main divisions of this chapter: (1) because of its origin and history Catholic NT scholarship in the U.S.A. has for the most part been mild and somewhat slow to come to grips with sensitive aspects of christology and ecclesiology; (2) we are still affected by a wrong understanding of how to relate biblical criticism to Church teaching.

A MILD NT CRITICISM SLOW TO FACE SENSITIVE ISSUES

Let me begin with some historical factors that have affected the quality of American Catholic NT scholarship.

1. The lack of a first-class American Catholic graduate biblical school. The problems of biblical scholarship are in part those of general Catholic theological education. In American Catholicism we have been insistent on teaching doctrine, religion, piety, and even "the faith"; but we have been slow in developing first-class graduate theological education. In particular, until recently there has been nowhere in the U.S.A. where a first-rate doctorate in biblical studies could be obtained under Catholic auspices. There are theology and religion departments in Catholic universities and colleges where Scripture is taught and where students can specialize in Scripture; but none of these can match the Protestant biblical departments of the best universities and divinity schools: Harvard, Yale, Union, Chicago, Duke, Princeton, etc. This has begun to change with the opening in 1976 of a Department of Biblical Studies at the Catholic University of America, with Joseph A. Fitzmyer, S.J., as one of the prominent professors. The Catholic University of America has long had a distinguished Department of Semitic Studies, so there are excellent resources there for the new department.

There is still a cloud on the horizon. In part, the slowness in developing Catholic graduate biblical schools in the U.S.A. has been caused by the rule that all Catholics who taught Scripture in seminaries and Catholic universities had to obtain a degree from either the Pontifical Biblical Institute or the Pontifical Biblical Commission in Rome. In the 1950s and 1960s when Catholic graduate students began going to the excellent Protestant biblical departments mentioned above, they had then to go off to Rome to get the extra Roman degree, which in many instances represented a level of training below that of the American degree they already possessed. (A Roman biblical doctorate is respectable, but the myth that it is the hardest degree in the world to get still has wide currency.) The cloud on the horizon that I mention is a recent attempt to reimpose the demand that all teachers of the Bible in seminaries and universities must have Roman degrees. If enforced, it will set back the development of a first-rate graduate American Catholic biblical school.

2. The antecedents of American Catholic NT scholarship before and during the Vatican Council. The formative influence on American Catholic NT studies in the 1950s was largely French. The changes in the Church's attitude toward the NT came at a time when Germany had not recovered from the War, and German Catholic criticism was underdeveloped. The great names of the times included Benoit and De Vaux in Jerusalem, and Lyonnet in Rome.[2] The

---

[2]An outstanding NT scholar was Msgr. L. Cerfaux of Louvain; however, relatively few American Catholic biblical scholars did their doctoral work at Louvain. An exception was R. G. Bandas in the early part of the century, and alas he turned extremely conservative in his last years.

French Catholic NT criticism of the 1950s was mild and very concerned to reconcile the new developments with scholastic theology and patristic authority. For that reason it made biblical criticism palatable in a conservative Catholic intellectual world.

The Vatican Council is sometimes romanticized as the high-water mark of Catholic biblical criticism; rather it was through the Council that bibilical criticism won *elementary* acceptance in Catholic circles, against a concerted attempt to undo the reforms of Pope Pius XII. Cardinal Bea who served as the biblical advisor of the dominant centrist forces at the Council had been known all his life as a very conservative scholar at the Biblicum in Rome; he was liberal only by contrast with the extremist forces that opposed him. The Council gave a public stage to the mild NT criticism of the 1950s, for an effort at popularization by English-speaking scholars did much to persuade the bishops that the Council should reject a fundamentalist approach to the Scriptures. Nevertheless, it should be mentioned that many of those who rendered this valuable service were men who sacrificed their scholarly careers to the task of popularization—they were not scholars known to the world at large or men who had published or would publish major works on the NT. Without their efforts, however, biblical criticism would not have survived in the Church.

Similarly the Pontifical Biblical Commission played a role at the Council. It is difficult to generalize, because at that time the Commission consisted of Cardinals, including some of the most conservative in the hierarchy (Ottaviani, Pizzardo, Ruffini), and its consultors ranged from the very conservative to the middle-of-the-road. But it was a group of the centrist consultors who shaped the 1964 Statement on the Historical Truth of the Gospels which became the backbone of *Dei verbum,* the 1965 Council constitution on revelation. This Statement (BRCFC 111–15) won for the Church the acceptance of a developmental approach to the Gospels, recognizing that the final Gospels go considerably beyond the ministry of Jesus and that later christology had been retrojected into the accounts of the ministry. This may have sounded radical at the time, but in fact the document was very moderate and avoided really thorny issues.

For instance, the P.B.C. statement speaks of Jesus as having "accommodated himself to the mentality of his listeners." This is a bland way of recognizing the limited theological worldview found in the Gospels, without confronting head-on the problem of the limited human knowledge of Jesus (see Chapter Five below). I want to emphasize that it would not have been in the interests of biblical scholarship at the Council to confront the thorny issues head-on. That would have supplied ammunition for our enemies. Yet, to be honest, I am not sure that those scholars present at the Council always saw the challenging implications of the new biblical criticism for doctrinal formulations—I was there and I certainly did not see all the implications I now see.

Protestant biblical scholarship was also present at the Council, and to many Catholics this seemed daring. To put the situation in focus, however, one needs to know something about the sector of Protestant biblical scholarship that came to the Council. To most Catholics, Oscar Cullmann was the best known of those present because he had done a book on Peter and was an ecumenist. I have always admired Cullmann and feel akin to directions in his thought; but I would not be objective if, in the spectrum of European Protestant scholarship, I did not place him right of center. In other words, the Protestant biblical scholarship at the Council stood at no great distance from its Catholic counterpart. (However, the history of the two scholarships was quite different; Catholics had moved considerably to the left to get to the right-of-center position where the Protestants already stood.) Nevertheless, even Cullmann complained about instances of a lack of biblical criticism in the Council documents, especially in relation to apostolic succession.[3] One can only speculate how much more severe the criticism would have been if any of the left-of-center Protestant biblical critics were present, e.g., Bultmann, Käsemann.

I have stressed this past history because frequently in the last

---

[3] O. Cullmann, *Dialogue on the Way* (Minneapolis: Augsburg, 1965), 138–40. He points out that Cardinal Bea was not able to remove some of the poor use of Scripture from the Council documents. "This way of citing biblical texts without taking into account the meaning of the context becomes even more questionable in view of the fact that there are certain theologically important declarations for which one would like to see the biblical basis. This is true of the principle of apostolic succession which is affirmed in several places in the schema."

fifteen years discussions have been marred by the misunderstanding that the Council gave Catholicism very advanced NT scholarship. Rather it met at a time when in many ways Catholic NT scholarship was just growing up. In a meeting at Notre Dame the year after the Council, George Lindbeck of Yale expressed the hope that Catholic biblical scholars would soon undertake the task of exposing the "questionable character" of the "irresponsible" exegesis that appeared, particularly in the Council documents on the Church and on Mary.[4]

In fact, the tone of post-conciliar Catholic NT scholarship is changing. There has been a massive re-entry of German Catholic scholars into the biblical field, and some of the younger Americans have been trained by them. Also many have gone to Johns Hopkins, Harvard, and Yale, and so the French-dominated scholarship of the pre-Vatican II period is beginning to seem dated. I hope that this will not lead to a patronizing attitude toward those who went before— without that pre-Vatican II scholarship, none of the present progress would have been possible. Rather it is a matter of regarding those predecessors as having built a lighthouse rather than a fence. Nevertheless, until the newer generation of scholars makes its very different approaches known through popularization, much of the Catholic discussion will be dominated by views that were popular at the time of the Council. Let me exemplify that in terms of outdated views of authorship and of insufficiently studied sensitive areas.

3. The currency of antiquated views about the authorship and dating of NT books. I have deliberately chosen my first examples of needed updating from an area in which Americans have traditionally not been overly interested, as having little relevance for Church problems. The only two major scholarly Catholic introductions to the NT that I know to have currency in the U.S.A. are by Wiken-hauser and by Robert and Feuillet, both of them pre-Conciliar in origin.[5] One is hard pressed to find in them a clear statement that in all

---

[4]In *Vatican II: An Interfaith Appraisal* (Univ. of Notre Dame Press, 1966), 223.

[5]Even though I am one of the editors of the *Jerome Biblical Commentary,* published shortly after the Council, I would have to state that commentary on and not introduction to the NT books is the strong point. (Many of the introductions simply

likelihood neither the Gospel of Matthew nor the Gospel of John was actually written by the apostle whose name it bears—a position held by almost all the major Catholic commentary writers today. But suppose one objects that, at least in a commentary like my own on John, or in John Meier's writings on Matthew, American Catholics could become aware of the majority scholarly position. I would answer by asking what does one do for Mark and Luke? In most discussions where these Gospels are invoked, there is not the slightest awareness of an authorship problem—with disastrous results when one tries to trace a historical development of christology and ecclesiology. (I remind my readers that I am talking about discussions among ordinarily well informed Catholics; technical scholars would, of course, know the problems.) In much popular Catholic writing on the NT, Papias' statement about Mark as the interpreter of Peter is quoted with the assumption that this Mark is the John Mark of Acts. Consequently there is a failure to recognize the extent to which this first written Gospel has already gone beyond the ministry of Jesus. In serious theological discussion in the last years I have seen both liberal and conservative arguments based on this, e.g., that Mark's less complimentary portrait of Peter is the historical one, that Mark's list of the Twelve must be accurate because they used to drop in at his mother's house in Jerusalem, that Jesus must have thought of the Twelve as priests because Mark says he *made* them be with him (the Greek OT speaks of "making" priests). I would regard such arguments as totally devoid of scientific value. The ecumenical study *Peter in the New Testament*[6] was quite right in refusing to base any conclusions on the Papias statement. Mark may be older than the other Gospels, but we know nothing biographical about the writer. And there is no way to demonstrate that he was directly dependent on any eyewitness preacher, e.g., on Peter. The reliability of Mark's tradition must be judged on its own merits, not on an assumption about its author.

---

copied "Bible of Jerusalem" positions.) On a popular level *Reading the New Testament* by Pheme Perkins (New York: Paulist, 1978) is better on introductory issues than the more scholarly books. There are, of course, good Protestant NT introductions available in English (e.g., that of W. G. Kümmel), but often these are suspect in the eyes of those who engage in inner Catholic Church discussions.

[6](New York: Paulist, 1973), 12²⁴.

The issue of the authorship of Luke's Gospel would be even more unfamiliar in ordinary Catholic theological discussion. The tradition that the author of Luke/Acts was Luke, the companion of Paul, is often fixed in popular Catholic writing in English, despite the clear mistakes that Acts make about the career of Paul. We see the implications of this position when a statement found in Acts 14:23, that Paul and Barnabas "appointed elders in every Church, with prayer and fasting," is used as an argument for the universal apostolic ordination of presbyters as early as the year 40! European Catholics are sometimes more fortunate; in Belgium, for instance, the leading Catholic expert on Acts, Jacques Dupont, makes clear in a popular journal[7] that the author is describing the church situation of his own time (several decades later) rather than the church situation of Paul's time; but one looks in vain in much American popular literature on Acts for that kind of guidance.

This brings us to the question of dating. In the two NT introductions cited above, one looks in vain for a clear statement of the deutero-Pauline status of the Pastoral Epistles (I–II Timothy, Titus), even though that position would be held by about eighty percent of worldwide Catholic scholarship. They may have been written by a Pauline disciple after Paul's lifetime, but not by Paul himself. We have no Catholic commentary on the Pastorals as critical in its scholarship as that of Norbert Brox (nor any studies of pseudepigraphy as thorough as his). Consequently, it is an uphill battle to get those discussing the origins of Christian ministry to see that, precisely because the practice of ministry in Paul's own time was *not* uniform, the author of the Pastorals has to invoke authority in order to regularize the appointing of presbyter-bishops in every town. He invokes the authority of Paul since he is sure that such a practice would represent his master's mind. I mention such an elementary example because, incredible as it seems, readers of the *Jerusalem Bible*[8] are told that the letters are written either by Paul or by a forger!

---

[7]*Assemblées du Seigneur* 26 (5th Sunday of Easter; 1973), 63–64.

[8]In the one volume edition, *The New Testament,* 263. (Seemingly the French original *épigone* is not so offensive as "forger.") It violates *elementary* scholarship to designate pejoratively as forgery the well attested biblical practice of attributing the works of disciples to their masters. See pp. 136–37 below.

If American Catholic popular literature on the Pauline Epistles shows no awareness of the majority scholarly position on the Pastorals, *a fortiori* the deutero-Pauline character of Colossians and Ephesians rarely colors ecclesiological discussions. Yet, increasingly, the majority view in Catholic scholarship seems to be moving toward the post-Pauline judgment, especially in the case of Ephesians. The relevance of the question for a picture of the first-century Church is clear. Many would think that it took about a third of a century (*ca.* 30–70) for the Church to become a separate institution from Judaism, one that had definitely broken away. But the objection is raised that Paul can scarcely have thought of the Church as still tied to Judaism because he speaks of the Church as the Body of Christ. Sometimes the objector does not realize what Msgr. Cerfaux clearly pointed out years ago, i.e., that the Church is *not* designated as the Body *of Christ* in the main Pauline Letters (I Corinthians, Romans). But the objection has some weight in regard to Colossians and Ephesians. The exaltation of the Church in those letters, not only as the Body of Christ, but also as the goal of salvation, implies a self-sufficiency of the Church in regard to Israel. That is one of the several reasons for arguing that Colossians and Ephesians belong to the 80s after the break with Judaism, rather than to the 60s.

I am not pretending that such "new" positions on dating are definitive. I myself have never been able to come to a definite position on Colossians. But what I am reporting is that there is little or no awareness of these problems in popular theological discussions about the origins of the Church or of the ministry on the American Catholic scene.

4. The failure to investigate sensitive areas. When I wrote my exploratory essay on "The Virginal Conception of Jesus" in 1971,[9] well-intentioned clergy, who were generally open to modern investigations, wondered was this not an area that should be avoided by Catholics, since any investigation of the difficulties, no matter how responsible, was certain to cause an uproar among ultraconservatives. To the contrary, I maintain that there is no area of Bible or of

---

[9]Subsequently published in VCBRJ 21–68.

doctrine related to the Bible that should not be studied in the light of modern biblical criticism. (Below I shall deal with responsibility to church authority.) Yet, in fact, there are very sensitive areas, crucial for christology and ecclesiology, that have not been discussed by Catholics on the American scene in a way that would contribute to theological growth.

Let me give one example. We saw above in Chapter One (p. 13) that the post-resurrectional "sayings" of Jesus may represent later community formulations. The risen Jesus gave his followers a commission, but perhaps not in words. As Christians came to understand the precise implications of that mission, *they* may have been the ones who phrased that understanding in words. Since we believe in the guidance of the Spirit for both the Church and the Scriptures, such a theory does not challenge these words as a *true* expression of the mind of the risen Jesus. However, if that expression came about only after years of Christian discovery and experience, the theory offers a definite challenge to what I have called "blueprint ecclesiology" (BRCFC 52–55) whereby Jesus is pictured as giving to his followers precise instructions about the Church, its future, and its structure. Approximately half the sayings crucial to blueprint ecclesiology are sayings of the risen Jesus, e.g., the mission to the Gentiles and the command to baptize in Matt 28:19, and the forgiveness and retention of sin in John 20:23. If, as I suggested in Chapter One, the Church came to understand such features only after years of being guided by the Spirit, a very different ecclesiology emerges. Not detailed answers given at the beginning, but answers discovered after problems were faced may be the model for understanding how God works through His Spirit. I shall return to this topic of blueprint ecclesiology in the next chapter when I discuss Jesus' limited knowledge of the future; but here I wish to emphasize the importance of the interpretation given to the sayings of the risen Jesus, and the crucial necessity for further critical investigation of these sayings. That is how NT criticism can make a substantial contribution to theological discussions.

RELATING BIBLICAL CRITICISM TO CHURCH DOCTRINES

Yet I am afraid that even were such an investigation made, many would see no relevance to important problems in christology, ecclesiology, etc.; for they do not have a proper understanding of the relationship between biblical scholarship and church doctrine. Once again I am speaking about the use of Scripture in intelligent theological discussion, and so I shall leave aside a number of simple difficulties, e.g., a failure to apply the proper theological notes to church statements, as if they were all infallible teaching, or a failure to recognize the historical conditioning of dogmatic statements. Nevertheless, even with a sophisticated understanding of dogma, there remain difficulties about the relationship between biblical criticism and church doctrine. Let me list three examples.

1. The attempt to solve modern critical problems on the basis of dogmatic statements phrased in a pre-critical era. These statements were phrased before the insight now accepted by the Church that the Gospels give a picture of Christ that goes considerably beyond the historical ministry of Jesus of Nazareth.[10] Therefore, such dogmatic statements do not necessarily refer to what Jesus did during his ministry; often they are a distillation from the whole NT picture and from the whole of first-century Christian history. Above (p. 40) I discussed this principle in relation to sacraments, but now let me discuss a more fundamental example. Does the doctrinal principle that Christ founded the Church settle the question of whether during his ministry Jesus spoke of the Church or thought in terms of the Church? There is only one passage in all four Gospels where Jesus speaks of the Church explicitly.[11] This is Matt 16:18 when he says, "You are Peter and upon this rock I shall build my Church." Theo-

---

[10]The 1964 statement of the Pontifical Biblical Commission (BRCFC 111–15) traces three stages in the formation of the Gospels, stretching from the historical ministry through a period of apostolic preaching to final writing by the evangelists. The document stresses how later insights and explanations became part of the Gospel narratives.

[11]The word *ekklēsia* occurs also in Matt 18:17, but there it refers to the local community, not to the Church as a whole.

logians of the past who reflected upon this statement had not the slightest idea that it might be a post-resurrectional statement retrojected into the ministry—a position now accepted by many Catholic and Protestant scholars, as may be seen in the ecumenical study *Peter in the New Testament.*[12] Moreover, theologians of the past often worked with the assumption that Matthew's was the oldest Gospel and that Matthew's scene (which is the only one to mention "Church") was the most complete version of what was said to Peter at Caesarea Philippi. Today, the majority of scholars would recognize that Mark is older than Matthew and that the sentence about building the Church upon Peter is a Matthean addition (from post-resurrectional material) to an account which originally lacked it, as we see in Mark and Luke. If this should be accepted, then there is no evidence that in the historical ministry Jesus ever spoke of the Church.

It may be objected that, even if Jesus did not use the word "Church," he surely thought of the reality of the Church. But that assertion depends for its validity on what we mean by "Church." There is Gospel evidence that Jesus called to himself a community of the renewed Israel, built around the Twelve who were to sit upon (twelve) thrones judging the twelve tribes of Israel (Matt 19:28; Luke 22:30). This is not too far from the notion of the renewed Israel found at Qumran. But the growth from Jesus' community of the renewed covenant to a Church separate from Judaism was a gradual happening in the post-resurrectional period, as described in Acts. Since we hold through faith that the Holy Spirit was at work in that growth, and since there was real continuity from the first stage to the last, there is no real difficulty with the affirmation that Christ founded the Church. But, as we have seen, such a doctrinal affirmation does not solve the problem of Jesus' intentions during his ministry. Let us move on to a related problem.

---

[12]Such a conclusion is in perfect harmony with the 1964 statement of the Pontifical Biblical Commission on the Historical Truth of the Gospels. There it is stated that the divinity of Jesus [which is what Peter has confessed] was perceived *after* the resurrection, and that the Christian preachers read that fuller understanding of Jesus back into their accounts of the words and deeds of Jesus.

2. *The forced interpretation of the silence of the NT in the light of later dogmatic interests.* Often in the NT there is little or no mention of a practice or a doctrine that later became a divisive issue in Christianity. In those forms of Christianity which claim to be true to the Bible alone, the silence of the NT *has* to be interpreted as favorable to the respective ecclesiastical position. But there has also been a tendency in Catholicism to insist that the silence must be interpreted in a way favorable to the Catholic doctrinal position, on the supposition that somehow that position would be endangered or weakened if it was not held by our NT forebears. This tendency may reflect a misunderstanding of the principle that revelation closed with the death of the last apostle. I, for one, have no difficulty with that principle if it is understood to mean that God gave us His Son as His ultimate self-revelation. The reason why the apostles are mentioned is the recognition that the mystery of Jesus was only poorly comprehended during his ministry, and that the apostolic penetration and proclamation of Jesus after the resurrection was an intrinsic stage of the revelation. I have great difficulty with the principle if revelation is confused with the formulation of revelation, and if the principle is taken to imply that the apostles or anyone else in the first century understood or formulated revelation completely. The urge to find the later formulations of revelation (church doctrines) as always somehow present in the wording of the NT is wrong in my opinion. Similarly wrong is the attitude that one should always interpret the silence of the NT in a way that favors such later formulations. I do not mean that one can or should interpret the silence so as to favor a position contradictory to later doctrine; but often the silence is indicative that the later doctrinal position or practice was not even an issue in NT times, and nothing favorable or contradictory can be presumed.

As an example, let me mention the Roman Catholic position that only a male ordained by a bishop through the laying-on of hands can validly celebrate the eucharist. Some want to argue that this was and even had to be the situation in NT times, and they would regard as disloyal (or worse) a Catholic exegete who finds no such regularity in the Scriptures. Yet the NT is virtually silent as to who celebrated the eucharist. There is *only one* relatively clear pertinent tradition, namely, the statement "Do this in commemoration of me," addressed to the apostles in Luke 22:19 (i.e., to the Twelve as we see from 22:30—the audience is vaguer in I Cor 11:25). This statement, which is notably absent in the Marcan/Matthean tradition, means that in the church tradition represented by Luke (and perhaps by Paul) there was a memory that the Twelve could and did celebrate the eucharist. Otherwise the NT gives us no definite information on the subject.[13] Yet many wish to assume from this silence that *only* those ordained by the apostles (or, more narrowly, by the Twelve) celebrated the eucharist in NT times. I would argue that such a position is no more loyal to later doctrine than is the contrary view. Later church practice of confining the celebration of the eucharist to the ritually ordained is a valid limitation no matter who celebrated the eucharist in NT times. The power to communicate the life and Spirit of Christ through visible signs was given to the Church in the person of the apostles, but the Church can administer these signs in any way that does not negate their original purpose. It was free to develop its own way of designating the celebrant of the eucharist; and indeed what more normal than that the Church found a clear and regular way of doing this only *after* a period of trial and unsuccessful experience?

If Catholic exegetes are freed from some supposed obligation to find the later custom in the NT and can interpret the first-century evidence for its own worth and not apologetically, we may see how unlikely is the thesis that only those manually ordained by the Twelve or even by the larger group of the apostles celebrated the eucharist. First, in the NT there are relatively few references to ordination or laying-on of hands for special ministries, and among them I know of no instance of ordination for the purpose of enabling people to administer sacraments. Second, we know of an apostolic foundation of relatively few communities (chiefly the Pauline); e.g., there is no NT evidence that apostles founded the Churches in Samaria, in

---

[13]Previously I was inclined to accept as eucharistic the statement in Acts 20:11 that Paul broke bread and ate. I am now rather inclined to think that Jacques Dupont is correct in maintaining (in private conversation) that this is not a reference to the eucharist, for then we would expect to hear that he broke bread and distributed it.

Antioch, or in Rome. Can we then realistically assume that there were present in every community, even those of non-apostolic foundation, celebrants of the eucharist ordained by the apostles? At the end of the first century *Didache* 10:7 instructs a community: "Let the prophets give thanks (*eucharistein*) as they will"—a suggestion that prophets celebrated the eucharist which may coincide with the evidence of Acts 13:1-2 that prophets celebrated the liturgy (*leitourgoun*) in the Church at Antioch. Can one really suppose that such a charismatic figure as the prophet was ordained by an apostle? Third, is not the insistence of Ignatius of Antioch (*ca.* 110) in *Smyrnaeans* 8:1 that only the bishop or his delegate can celebrate the eucharist more intelligible if he is arguing for a discipline recently introduced, rather than for a universally acknowledged practice three-quarters of a century old? A discipline fixed since apostolic times would scarcely have needed the intensive backing that Ignatius gives it. Thus, I contend that it is a misuse of the argument from silence to assume that the first-century custom had to be the same as the later custom—there is no doctrinal need to do so and most of our information points in the opposite direction. Those who want to base the legitimacy of the Catholic priesthood on such dubious assumptions from silence expose us to the justified distrust of our fellow Christians.

3. The tendency to neglect or underplay texts that do not accord with later dogmatic positions. Related to the problem of silence is the more difficult problem of attitudes in the NT that are contrary (notice, I do not say contradictory) to later positions. Some can understand how the Church may have moved from silence to a new affirmation or practice, but their understanding of inspiration makes them very uneasy about the existence of a movement in the NT which began in a contrary direction from later church positions. I suggested in Chapters One and Two that such an approach involves a misunderstanding of inspiration and inerrancy, for a larger conception of biblical meaning recognizes that tension can exist between what the author meant and what the Bible now means in the Church. Just as the Church is justified in proclaiming an afterlife even though Job 14:13-22 rejected it (while other biblical authors accepted it), so can the Church later teach doctrinally something that an individual NT author, in passing, seems not to have accepted.[14] We would simply have to say that the NT author, not having reflected in depth on a point (which was probably not an issue at the time), took a wrong position, and that later Christianity reached a deeper insight, in fidelity to other biblical views.

As an example, let me mention the Roman Catholic devotion for Mary, a devotion that I earnestly hope we never lose. But I see no challenge to Catholic mariology if an individual NT author did not have that devotion and indeed betrays no real esteem for Mary. I think Catholic exegetes have to face that possibility honestly and not write books on Mary which concentrate only on the NT passages (mostly from Luke and John) that give evidence of an emerging symbolic theology of Mary and which neglect earlier passages that point in a contrary direction.[15] We Catholics have not accepted biblical criticism if we cannot deal honestly with the unfavorable view of Jesus' natural family (including Mary) in Mark 3:21–35 and 6:1–6. In 3:21 we are told that Jesus' "own" (relatives) thought he was beside himself and set out to seize him. Ten verses later Mark reports that Jesus' mother and his brothers came and asked for him. Mark may well have joined two once separate scenes (and so originally Jesus'

---

[14]Notice that I say "in passing." In my mind there would be a theological problem were the Church to affirm a position contradictory to a major, formal teaching of a NT author. The relation of the passing opinions of an OT author to subsequent Christian teaching may be different from the relation of the opinions of a NT author to subsequent Christian teaching. New revelation separates the OT author from Christianity; a deepening insight into the same revelation separates the NT author from later Christian position. If I understand Catholic thought correctly, "contradictory" could be applied to the former relationship but not to the latter, whence my insistence on not going beyond "contrary" in reference to the NT.

[15]I find seriously defective two recent works: M. Miguens, "Mary a Virgin?", a book length article in *Marian Studies* 26 (1975), 26–179 (which was later published as a book and vigorously criticized, as I reported on p. 28 above); and J. McHugh, *The Mother of Jesus in the New Testament* (Garden City: Doubleday, 1975). The former uses Mark's failure to mention Joseph to prove that Mark knew of the virginal conception; the latter uses Mark to prove that the "brothers" of Jesus were not Mary's children—neither really wrestles with the evidence that Mark seems to include Mary among those relatives of Jesus who thought he was beside himself and who paid him no honor.

mother may not have been among "his own"—see John 7:3–5 where only Jesus' brothers are involved). Yet the sequence indicates that *Mark judged* that Jesus' mother was among "his own" and that she thought he was beside himself—scarcely a graceful picture of Mary. Moreover, in 3:31–35 Mark has Jesus make a sharp distinction between the physical family of mother and brothers standing outside and a family of brother, and sister, and mother constituted by disciples who do the will of God, a family already seated inside with Jesus. One may conclude from this that Mark did not think that Mary and the brothers were disciples of Jesus during his ministry—a conclusion strengthened by the fact that the Marcan Jesus complains in 6:4 that a prophet is without honor *among his own relatives* and in his own house.

Subsequent developments in NT thought moved in a direction different from Mark's. It has been customary in Catholic exegesis to force Mark's texts into agreement with the theology of Matthew and Luke. However, the most eloquent refutation of that exegesis is the fact that both Matthew and Luke (who knew of the virginal conception and favored Mary) had to change the offending Marcan statements. Neither Matthew nor Luke reports that Jesus' "own" thought he was beside himself or has him complain that a prophet is without honor among his own relatives.[16] In addition, Luke modifies the scene where the mother and brothers come and ask for Jesus. In Luke 8:19–21 no longer are the mother and brothers set over against the family of Jesus' disciples; rather they are included in it: "My mother and my brothers are those who hear the word of God and do it." Luke has developed a major interest in Mary as the first disciple who heard the word of God and did it (1:38); she was present at the beginning of the proclamation of the Gospel and at the beginning of the Church (Acts 1:14). As a Catholic I would say that the Lucan direction is the correct direction for the future of the Christian community, but that should not cause me to force Mark into a similar thought pattern.

*   *   *

[16]The way that Matthew and Luke excise the Marcan statements is the best proof that Miguens is wrong and that Mark's attitude toward Mary is irreconcilable with a knowledge of the virginal conception.

I shall end my remarks with that last example of how the freedom of NT exegesis should not be constrained by a wrong understanding of the implications of dogma. In the next chapter I shall argue even more strongly that the way we present doctrine cannot ignore the discoveries of NT exegesis. If dogmatic formulations are historically conditioned and sometimes need to be reformulated, as *Mysterium Ecclesiae* maintains (BRCFC 116–18), biblical criticism must make its contribution to the reformulation—a reunderstanding that has to be approved by Church authority, to be sure, but a reunderstanding in which exegetes should have a consultative role. As I mentioned in Chapter Two, there are those in the Church who charge that biblical criticism is barren and that we need a more spiritual reading of the Bible. Criticism may be barren in the hands of certain practitioners, but some who make the charge would dearly like to distract Catholics from a frank and honest discussion of the origins of Christianity and the challenging implications of those origins for bringing about change in the Church of today. I think of at least three other moments in church history when biblical criticism began to make an appearance in Roman Catholic theology—in the latter years of the life of St. Jerome when he finally broke away from the allegory of Origen; in the twelfth century when the school of St. Victor in Paris revived language study and the importance of the literal sense; and in the beginnings of pentateuchal criticism under Richard Simon. In each of those instances biblical criticism was suffocated by pietism and exaggerated traditionalism, ultimately on the grounds that it could not be right because it differed from what Catholics had been saying before. Far from thinking that biblical criticism is barren, I think it has only begun to have its impact on the Catholic Church scene. It must not be suffocated again by a desire to preserve the *status quo.* In particular, Catholic NT criticism, as it begins to be more trenchant than was possible in the period of the Council, must draw out honestly the implications of its observations for theology and ecclesiology and ecumenism. It has the power to serve as the conscience of the Church by reminding us what it was like when men and women first began to follow the Lord Jesus Christ.

Chapter Five
MOVING ALL CHRISTIANS
TO THINK

Summary of the theme:[1] *Biblical studies have implications not only for the general position and direction of the Church but also for the way individuals understand Christianity. While it is difficult to reach all Christians, large numbers are engaged in one way or another in teaching religion. An application of modern biblical insight to two of the most frequently taught doctrines (creation, humanity/divinity of Jesus), taken by way of examples, results in profound implications for the way Christians think.*

In the preceding chapter I discussed biblical scholarship in its benevolent role of challenging the Church and moving it slowly but ultimately to be what it should be. This challenge may first reach perceptive church leaders; but eventually it must reach all in the Church, moving Christians to be what they should be. This is an immense task; but here, as a gesture in that direction, let me show how biblical criticism can affect one very important group of Christians—

---

[1]The material represented in this chapter was originally delivered at the 78th annual convention of the National Catholic Educational Association at New York City, on April 22, 1981, under the title: "Difference of Thought as a Constructive Christian Force—a Biblical View." It was published in *Origins* 10 (#47, May 7, 1981) 737–43, as "The Importance of How Doctrine is Understood"; and in CM 79 (June 1981) 8–18, as "Doctrinal Diversity and the Thinking Christian."

those involved in teaching Christian doctrine to others. The formal religious education of Roman Catholics before 1970 was entrusted largely to clergy and religious. Since then, partly because of the decline of numbers among clergy and religious, and partly because of the closing of Catholic schools, much of the educational task has been passed on to the laity. A primary concern of the hierarchy responsible for religious education was to be certain that Christian doctrine would continue to be taught, a concern which has meant the approval of textbooks and the basic certification of a new generation of teachers who were not the products of seminaries, convents, or scholasticates. In this chapter I assume all that and wish to push farther to the opportunity offered by these events for the religious education of those who are called upon to be teachers of religion—in short, what teaching can mean for the teacher as a Christian.

As we look back upon the second thousand years of Christianity, Vatican Council II is rivaled only by the Reformation (plus the Council of Trent) in the changes of thought it has made in Western Christianity where the Bishop of Rome is the most prominent religious figure. Like the sixteenth-century upheaval, Vatican II has affected both those who continue to accept the pope's authority and those who do not. The changes have been so sweeping that the re-education of Catholics has become a necessity to counter confusion, misunderstanding, and resistance.[2] This need has generally been recognized. Renewal or updating sessions, study sabbaticals, summer programs and religious education congresses have been made available. Nevertheless, while these have helped a respectable percentage of clergy and religious, the numbers of the laity are so large that what can be done in lectures and courses is only "a drop in the bucket." For religious educators there is a need to stress the possibility of self-education through teaching; and here I plan to concentrate on the possibility of becoming a thinking Christian through one's understanding of what is to be taught, especially as that is influenced by a modern approach to the Bible.

Rightly has it been proclaimed that a major goal in religious

---

[2]Catholics over 30–35 years of age would have had their basic religious formation before the influence of Vatican II was felt, while most younger Catholics would have been taught by teachers in the over-30 range.

education is the communication of doctrine to pupils (in order to provide a basis for Christian living). Rightly, too, church leaders have been solicitous about the doctrinal content of courses and textbooks. But sometimes it has not been emphasized that Christians, whether pupils or teachers, have their *religious outlook shaped not only or even primarily by the doctrine itself but by the way the doctrine is understood.* Some church authorities thought that they could satisfy complaints about the lack or loss of doctrinal content (complaints at times justified[3]) by supplying a list of basic teachings, only to find ultraconservatives retorting that this was not enough since these lists did not specify the right way of understanding doctrines! In underlining the difference between doctrine and a way of understanding the doctrine, let me insist that, whether or not those involved recognize it, there are *no major differences between the Catholic center and the Catholic right in matters of official Catholic doctrine.*[4] But there are sharp differences in the way doctrines are understood, and the right wing generally argues that its understanding of doctrine *is* doctrine. (Often the rightist understanding is arrogantly entitled "orthodox" with the not-too-subtle implication that any other interpretation is heterodox or heretical.) Let me illustrate my contention from two doctrines that have biblical roots, namely, the creation of the world and the two natures of Jesus Christ. I am deliberately choosing one doctrine that many Catholics have already thought about because it

---

[3]The influence of liberalism was seen, at times, in a curriculum that concentrated on moral attitudes with the supposition that doctrinal content would be learned later.

[4]I shall give little attention here to a Catholic left wing which does not seem constrained by dogma. Yet let me make two observations. First, a relatively small portion of the Catholic left consists of those who have detailed knowledge of past doctrines which they now reject. (Of course, rightist extremists will regard the large centrist body of Catholic theologians as denying doctrine, despite clear affirmations to the contrary; but that demonstrates only that if one's stance is far enough to the right, everyone else is automatically to the left.) The larger portion of the left consists of those whose opinions represent a denial of doctrine that they have never examined or debated in detail. Second, the left, whether professionally learned or instinctive, is not likely to gain much influence on the American hierarchy or on the mass of Catholic people. The prevailing mood is conservative, and the real issue is whether the conservatism will be moderate (centrist) or extremist (rightist).

is frequently in the press, and another doctrine the implications of which may be less familiar.

DIFFERENT BIBLICAL UNDERSTANDINGS OF THE SAME DOCTRINES

Both Catholic center and Catholic right agree on *the doctrine of creation:* God created all things. Often the Catholic right (like Protestant fundamentalists) will insist that this implies a literal interpretation of the Genesis story, namely, creation in six days or six periods of time; human beings did not evolve from lower species; woman was formed from man's body; life was in an idyllic state. The Catholic center will tend to think that the doctrine of creation tells us nothing about time periods or evolution, which are matters for investigation by science. The role of God as creator is the central affirmation guaranteed by revelation, no matter the time or manner of what happened.[5] In this view, the author of Genesis had no revelation about the precise beginnings of the world and of life, but shared the prescientific views of his time, which we now know to have been inaccurate, even if we cannot be absolute about what did happen.

Both Catholic center and Catholic right agree on *the doctrine of the two natures of Jesus Christ* in the sense that he was truly divine and truly human. Often the Catholic right will insist that the divinity of Jesus means that there could have been no limitations during his earthly life, i.e., in his humanity he knew the future in detail, he could express fully his own divine identity and he could define all the doctrines of Christian revelation (e.g., Trinity, sacraments). The Catholic center tends to see no contradiction between Jesus' divinity and his having human limitations (except sin—the one exemption from humanity that NT authors agree upon), so that Jesus could be tempted, could learn obedience, would express his ideas in the thought-world of first-century Judaism, need not have known the fu-

---

[5]It is regrettable that the communications media have been allowed to create a dualism dubbed "creationist" and "evolutionist," as if belief in creation forced one to accept Genesis literally and to deny evolution.

ture and need not have been able to formulate doctrines of the subsequent Greco-Latin Church.

In my judgment the two understandings of doctrine that I am calling rightist and centrist are perfectly tolerable within the sphere of orthodox Roman Catholicism.[6] Since I have warned that the right wing tends to think of its understanding as doctrinal, let me caution further against the rightist tendency to cite as support church statements without proper discrimination. Three factors need to be remembered in this regard: (1) Statements collected from popes and from various types of councils are often of uneven authority, and their binding force can be decided only by extremely careful theological analysis. Some statements represent merely pious opinion; some express the common theories of the period in which they were formulated; some represent the majority opinion of theologians over the ages; some are defined matters of faith. Such differentiation of authority is no modern innovation; it has for centuries been an elementary principle enunciated in the theological textbooks. (2) Even in the case of statements with greater authority, their background must be carefully analyzed and investigated in order to know what precisely was being affirmed. For instance, if I may return to the subject I discussed in Chapter Two (p. 40 above), a knowledge of theological history would make it clear that the doctrinal statement, "Jesus Christ instituted seven sacraments," tells us how many sacred actions are to be regarded as not merely of church origin but as essential to communicating and maintaining the eternal life brought by Jesus Christ. They were instituted by him in the sense that they are part of the mission he gave to proclaim the kingdom. One who does not investigate the history of the doctrine might conclude wrongly that it tells us that the earthly Jesus had a clear notion of sacrament as we have come to understand it, and that *he* thought explicitly of

---

[6]Examples of left-wing treatments of the two doctrines that could be considered heterodox would be: (a) that no special action of God need be posited in the beginnings of the world or of a truly human species; (b) that Jesus' limitations imply that he only *became* divine during the course of his earthly ministry. See the Roman Doctrinal Congregation's declaration on the incarnation in February 1972 (*Mysterium Filii Dei*).

seven such sacraments![7] (3) Even the doctrinal statements of the Church are, in a sense, time-conditioned. It is significant how seldom right-wing spokesmen quote a crucially important passage from *Mysterium Ecclesiae* (BRCFC 116–18), the 1973 declaration of the Roman Doctrinal Congregation (Holy Office). This declaration affirms that sometimes the dogmatic formulas of the Church are formulated in terms that bear traces of "the changeable conceptions of a given epoch" and solve only certain questions, and then incompletely. Hence these formulas may need to give way to new expressions.

A proper application of the three factors I have just mentioned means that in relation to the doctrines of creation and of the two natures of Christ, no matter how many past ecclesiastical statements are brought forward by those who insist on the rightist interpretation of the doctrines,[8] *today the centrist position is securely within the boundaries of Catholic thought loyal to the magisterium.* The failure

---

[7]In the Western Church the number of sacraments was still a matter of lively debate 1,000 years after Christianity began, with a medieval consensus finally being reached on seven.

[8]Let me illustrate the problem with one example. Past church statements affirm that Christ had the Beatific Vision during his ministry, but it is irresponsible to bring them into the modern discussion of Jesus' knowledge without alerting people to two facts: (a) The theory of Jesus' Beatific Vision was advanced in the Middle Ages as an answer to a problem: Although one could *not* suppose that the divine (nonconceptual) knowledge of the Second Person of the Trinity was functional in the human mind of Jesus (which operated with concepts), the Gospels portray him as having extraordinary knowledge about God, the future, etc.—might he not have had the Beatific Vision which gave him such knowledge? However, now the Church (Pontifical Biblical Commission, 1964) has officially explained that the Gospels do not give us literal accounts of the ministry of Jesus, but narratives into which the post-resurrectional theological insights of the Christian preachers have been read back. (For the text, see BRCFC 113, VIII). In fidelity to this church statement, a Catholic may maintain that a true post-resurrectional insight into Jesus' extraordinary identity as Son of God has been given expression in the Gospels in terms of extraordinary knowledge during the ministry. This theory obviates the need of positing Jesus' Beatific Vision. (b) Accordingly, many of the most respected Catholic theologians today, including Rahner, Ratzinger, Lonergan, and von Balthasaar, have reinterpreted the theory of Jesus' Beatific Vision without producing any indication of ecclesiastical disapproval. (Some of these theologians wisely posit Jesus' nonconceptual awareness of His divine self through the hypostatic union.)

to take into account such factors explains why rightists are angry with the bishops or even with Rome[9] for not condemning centrists who in their judgment are denying past statements of the Church. Occasionally, of course, blindness in this matter is almost willful, as when the 1955 statement of the Secretary of the Pontifical Biblical Commission (BRCFC 110–11) that Catholics have "full freedom" with regard to past decrees of that Commission is dismissed as without authority.

THE IMPORT OF SUCH DIFFERENCES FOR CHRISTIANS

But now the important question that is the central concern of this chapter: *If two such diverse understandings of doctrine, rightist and centrist, are tolerable within the bonds of Catholic orthodoxy, what difference does it make which view one holds?* I would reply that it makes an enormous difference in the way one thinks as a Christian. To illustrate this I am now going to take the two doctrines—first, that of creation, and second, that of the two natures—and draw out the implications of the rightist and centrist interpretations in terms of the way the respective Christian will think.

Let us begin with the implications of the way one understands creation: (1) The rightist and centrist interpretations will produce very different attitudes toward science. Even if geology and paleontology leave gaps in our knowledge of cosmic and human origins, they certainly substantiate a more complex situation than that derived from the literalist interpretation of Genesis. The holder of the rightist view of creation will be threatened and placed on the defensive by every new discovery that lengthens the age of the earth or supports an evolutionary picture. True, scientists must not be allowed to "pontificate" about theological issues that lie beyond the competency of their specialization; but it is another matter for religious people to be battling constantly against observations that are properly within the scope of science, such as the date and classification of geological formations and fossils. It is embarrassing to see

---

[9]Now that Pope Paul VI is dead, he is frequently described in rightist circles as having been too weak or vacillating in cracking down on the Catholic "left" (read "center").

rightists lionizing the maverick scientist whose views can be used to challenge the overwhelming scholarly consensus in favor of human evolution. The centrist, on the other hand, who holds that Genesis tells us nothing doctrinal about either the time or manner of creation, can be relaxed about pertinent scientific discoveries, for they can constitute no challenge to the understanding that God was behind whatever happened. To my mind the attitude toward science is crucial in Christianity's role in the modern world. When in the course of history Christianity has been at its best, it has been able to digest and profit from every new major body of knowledge it encountered. For example, it profited from Platonic philosophy in the early patristic centuries, from Aristotelianism and the Arab sciences in the Middle Ages, and from the rediscovery of Greco-Roman classics in the Renaissance. But in the last few centuries, only after kicking and screaming have Christians made a reluctant compromise with great bodies of new knowledge in the physical sciences, sociology, medicine, and psychology. Too often the first Christian reaction has been to condemn pioneers in each field as holding views contrary to divine revelation, and only later to acknowledge that revelation did not settle the scientific issue and that a more subtle understanding of doctrine could allow acceptance of the new proposal formerly condemned. The centrist view of creation, which makes Christians less tense about the conclusions of science, should incline them to withhold condemnatory judgments in other areas where there develop apparent conflicts between past doctrinal positions and new scientific discoveries.

(2) The presupposition of the rightist view of creation is that we can and must go on reading Genesis literally in the manner of our ancestors in the faith. The centrist view presupposes that we can change our interpretation of Genesis and implicitly that our Christian ancestors were wrong when they thought that the doctrine of creation told them the time and manner of cosmic and human origins. In other words, the centrist Christian is led to realize that what was once thought to be doctrine can later be discovered not to be doctrine. (This does not mean that infallibility ought to be rejected. It means that, as the Roman Doctrinal Congregation affirmed when defending infallibility in *Mysterium Ecclesiae,* one must be careful in

diagnosing the exact point of a doctrine, and that even then a doctrine does not solve all questions pertinent to the issue.) This should make the centrist Christian more cautious on other doctrinal issues in our time when it is claimed that a new position is not reconcilable with revelation as it has been understood in the past. He or she will be more inclined to reexamine past doctrinal statements to see whether the new position might clarify the real point of the revelation.

(3) The rightist view of creation that is based on a literal interpretation of Genesis implies a stance about revelation itself. The author of Genesis was scarcely present when the world and the human race were created; and he would scarcely have had access to an exact tradition coming down from the time of those events, thousands or millions of years ago. Therefore, in order for him to know the exact process of creation, God would have had to reveal to him all the details. Almost surely, then, in the rightist interpretation revelation involves God's pouring bodies of information into the human mind, and giving a precise picture of the past (or even of the future, if we consider other parts of the Bible literally interpreted). The centrist view of creation implies quite another approach to revelation. The author shared the prescientific views of his age about the manner of cosmic and human origins and received no bodies of new information from God. But God did lead him to understand that nothing existed which had not been created by God and that, as they were created, all things were good—human beings were responsible for sin. Revelation is thus conceived as a divine communication received in and through the author's perception of God's relation to the world around him. The style of communication between God and the author loses part of that aura of the marvelous[10] which causes some to think (wrongly, in my judgment) that the people of the Bible were different from all the people who have existed since and that the biblical God continually acted in a way that He has not

---

[10]The notion of God's speaking in revelation is too often understood in a simplistic manner. One may confine divine revelation uniquely to the biblical period without extending that uniqueness to a marvelous manner of communication. See Chap. 1 above.

followed since. I think that such an attitude imperils the pedagogic value of the Bible.

I have been drawing out some of the implications of the rightist and centrist views of creation; let me now do the same in the question of the limitations of Jesus' human knowledge. (4) The view taken of Jesus' knowledge has implications for how Christians relate themselves to the incarnation. The rightist theory of unlimited knowledge greatly reduces the *kenōsis* or emptying involved in the incarnation. Uncertainty about the future and about how some of the most urgent issues in life will turn out is one of the greatest agonies of being human. The Jesus who knew exactly what would happen becomes almost a play actor on the stage of time, unaffected by vicissitudes. He is a Jesus who should not have feared death in Gethsemane since he knew exactly how he would triumph, and he should not have found it necessary to pray that this cup pass from him.[11] One may ask whether he would have been truly human like us in all things but sin (Council of Chalcedon). The centrist view, which allows human limitations (except sin), inevitably takes the lowly side of the incarnation more seriously. Jesus would share in the human anguish of not knowing exactly how what he had begun would triumph. Triumph it would, but that was a matter of trusting the Father. The length of time before the triumph, its manner and extent would not have been known to Jesus during his ministry, and so death would have come as an enemy to be overcome through complete self-abandonment to the Father's plan—a plan not clear to the human mind of the Son (Mark 13:32). The incarnate Son who emerges from the centrist view of human limitations is one who emptied himself, took on the form of a servant and became obedient even to death on a cross (Philip 2:7–8). This difference between the rightist and centrist views of Jesus' humanity affects its exemplary character. We can admire a Jesus without limitations, but then we do not have the inspiration of a Jesus who is able "to sympathize with our

---

[11]I remind the reader that I am discussing the implications of a theory that is possible *within the range of doctrine;* but biblical criticism might reduce to marginal the possibility to be accorded to this theory.

weaknesses" because "in every respect he has been tempted as we are" (Heb 4:15).

(5) In Chapter Four above, in discussing the issue of whether the sayings of the *risen* Jesus were actually spoken by him or formulated afterwards through early church experience guided by the Spirit, I pointed out the ramifications of this for a blueprint theory of church formation. Similarly, a major implication of the two views of Jesus' human knowledge *during his public ministry* concerns the way in which the foundation of the Church is understood. The rightist view whereby Jesus foresaw the future in detail will assume almost inevitably that Jesus had a precise ecclesiastical plan or blueprint, e.g., how the Church would come about and in what direction it would grow; the conversion of the Gentiles; church organization, including papacy, episcopacy and priesthood; the seven sacraments and what was required for their validity. The centrist view in which Jesus had no such detailed future knowledge will understand his foundation of the Church in another way: he left behind the disciples whom he had called; to them both in his ministry and after the resurrection he gave a mission to proclaim the kingdom; he also gave them a Spirit. Under the influence of that Spirit, as they encountered problems, they developed responses (e.g., in terms of deciding to convert Gentiles and of structuring the Church); they also gradually uncovered visible ways of celebrating the gift of God's grace pertinent to various aspects of Christian life—sacramental actions related to what Jesus had done in his ministry.[12] The rightist view, then, will interpret church development against the background of detailed directives that Christians had to follow obediently; but the centrist view implies much creative interaction between new problems and a guiding Spirit. The rightist view allows little freedom to restructure and little adaptability to new demands. The centrist view, while recognizing that history and past decisions limit options so that all changes are not possible, has a much freer estimate of how the Church can adjust in function and form to new circumstances. The centrist view will also have a greater appreciation of the possibilities offered by unfore-

---

[12]These sacraments involved Christ's Spirit and his grace, and they concretized the mission he gave. Therefore, in a very real way the sacraments were of Christ's institution and not simply of church institution.

seen challenges. Such challenges are not welcome in a blueprint outlook, for they threaten to undermine what has been laid out with
care and foresight. But in a centrist view, challenges offer the Spirit
the opportunity to lead the Church in new directions, and often it is
in dialogue with challenges that the Church hears its Master's voice.

*   *   *

I have now finished discussing how two Catholic doctrines may
be understood in different biblical ways and the implications of those
different understandings for one's vision of Christianity. Some regard
it as a scandal that because of biblical criticism there are diverse
ways of understanding doctrine and would beg church authority to
exclude any interpretation different from their own. I think that the
emergence of new ways of understanding traditional doctrine (carefully reasoned and documented ways, however, and not just vague
impressions about what doctrine might mean) has been one of the
most exciting and fruitful phenomena in twentieth-century Catholicism, enriching the Church and giving Christians a chance to think.
Look at the range of possibilities opened by the centrist understanding of just the two doctrines we have discussed, namely: *that* revelation need not be seen as a collection of answers supplied by God in
all the complex areas of human experience, past and present; *that* in
the human struggle to understand God's communication and to
phrase His revelation as doctrine, there is an ongoing process of
sharpening by rethinking and rephrasing under the impact of new
questions; *that* an openness to scientific discoveries is in our times
one of the principal ways in which we can make our contribution to
rethinking doctrine; *that* the exemplary character of the humanity of
Jesus may be serving more effectively as revelation now because we
realize the extent to which God's Son shared our limitations; and
consequently *that* Jesus' founding of the Church need not have been
specific in many details and may have left to Christians guided by
the Spirit considerable freedom and adaptability.[13] And I have insist-

---

[13]In Catholic thought the magisterium has the final role in deciding when and if
major adaptations are acceptable.

ed that such insights flow from understandings of doctrine that are perfectly within the boundaries of Catholic orthodoxy. Fidelity to Catholic doctrine is not narrow or confining and, when understood properly, allows plenty of room to think.

But how available to the ordinary teacher is such a way of re-thinking biblically basic Christian attitudes? Obviously, scholarship is required for developing sound new interpretations of doctrine,[14] but one does not need to be a scholar to profit from this development. In the examples we have been discussing, teachers of religion who take the trouble to read any one of a number of basic texts on creation or on Jesus' humanity would find the centrist views I described above. Those views might well differ from what they had learned when they went to school (depending on when that was), but the footnotes would tell such teachers that the new positions are held by numerous scholars who are in good standing with the Church.[15] The difficult task may be that of getting teachers to think through the implications of an older and of a newer interpretation of doctrine in the manner I have tried to illustrate. That process can constitute for teachers a remarkable self-education in the Catholicism of the post-Vatican II period. Teaching of its very nature should involve the repetition of the intelligent views held by others, past and present; but only when the implications of those views have been thought through can conviction and enthusiasm be gained as to why the issues should be important both to the teacher and the pupil.

Finally, however, I would stress that this "thinking through" is necessary for the teacher not only as teacher but also as Christian. I have insisted that both rightist and centrist interpretations of doctrine are orthodox. Therefore, rightists have no right to attack centrists as heretics or modernists, and centrists have no right to despise

---

[14]As indicated in the preceding footnote, church authorities have the ultimate right and duty to reject a new interpretation as unacceptable. However, it is not true that one cannot work with new interpretations of doctrine proposed by respectable scholars until the magisterium has spoken, for often it never speaks. Indeed, most re-interpretations find tacit rather than explicit acceptance by the Church. Church authorities understand quite well that to be silent over a long period about what most theologians are saying is ultimately to consent: *tacēre est consentire.*

[15]R. McBrien, *Catholicism* (Minneapolis: Winston, 1980), is almost an encyclopedia of this type of information.

rightists as Neanderthal Catholics. But I cannot pretend that the religious stances produced by (or reflective of) the two interpretations would be equally open to receiving a Christ who asked disturbing questions, whose whole spirit was one of rethinking the presuppositions of the Judaism of his time, and who consequently was offensive to religious people. The basic issue for the future of the Church may not be whether both rightist and centrist views are loyally Catholic (they are) or whether they are truly religious (they are), but to what extent their implications *are Christian* in the sense of opening those who hold them to a Christ who proclaimed: "Change your minds, for the kingdom of heaven is at hand."[16]

---

[16]Matt 4:17 (see Mark 1:15; Acts 2:38). The Greek verb *metanoein,* from its component parts, would mean "to think over"; for the basic component is *noein,* "to perceive, gain insight, think," related to *nous,* "mind" (cf. English "noetic"). For sinners, changing one's mind or rethinking involves repenting or changing one's life; for religious people not conscious of sin, the demand of *metanoein* might better be translated literally as change of mind. If one reflects upon the opposition encountered by Jesus' demand, the Gospels record little rejection of him by sinners, but much rejection by those whom he challenged to change their religious outlook.

Chapter Six
AN EXAMPLE:
RETHINKING THE PRIESTHOOD
BIBLICALLY FOR ALL

Summary of the theme:[1] *Besides affecting the way individuals understand Christianity, biblical studies touch on Christian spiritual life. For example, "priesthood" in the Scriptures is applicable not only to those formally involved in cult, but to all God's people, and primarily to Christ. Each of these different biblical concepts of priesthood has its own strengths and ideals, so that they complement each other in the total Christian picture.*

We have seen some changes of outlook and thought that might result under the impact of biblical criticism as traditional Christian doctrines are considered in a new way. Yet, in a sense, all the changes for the Church and for Christians thus far described are cerebral. I must emphasize that modern approaches to the Bible have an impact as well on the spiritual life. Let me illustrate in terms of a very sacred concept, the priesthood. Many would regard that as a

---

[1]The material represented in this chapter was originally delivered at St. Mary's Seminary, Baltimore, the oldest (1791) and for many years the largest of American Catholic seminaries. The occasion (October 1, 1979) was the fiftieth anniversary of the relocation of the seminary in new buildings in the Roland Park section of the city. It was published in CM 78 (March 1980) 11–20 as "The Challenge of the Three Biblical Priesthoods"; and in *Emmanuel* 86 (June 1980) 314–22.

topic that concerns only the clergy; but when we look at the Bible critically, it soon becomes apparent that priesthood involves all Christians and every aspect of Christian life. Indeed, there are three priesthoods contained in the biblical pictures of Israel and Christianity; and when they are examined, each of them has spiritual meaning for Christians in general and for Roman Catholics in particular.

THE FIRST PRIESTHOOD

I would begin with the priesthood which should always be thought of first, even though we do not always do so. It is the priesthood of which the Epistle to the Hebrews writes eloquently, the priesthood of Jesus Christ. This is a priesthood that is unique, that is sovereign and that he can share with no one, the priesthood of the divine Son. I often wonder why it does not have more impact on church thought. I know why it did not have more impact in antiquity: that was because the Epistle to the Hebrews that writes so eloquently of it did not find its way into the canon of the NT for hundreds of years and so was not a major formative force in early Christian thought. Particularly in the Western Church, Hebrews was very slow to receive acceptance as Scripture. And yet, the unknown author—surely not Paul—was perhaps the most balanced and careful theologian in the NT in his appreciation of Jesus as God and man, calling him God, yet specifying that he was like us in everything except sin, a rare combination that the Church has struggled with ever since. This author also understood the uniqueness of Christ's priesthood; for he insists that while the former priests were many in number, Christ is the only priest, nay high priest, of the New Covenant. By a single offering, Christ has perfected for all time those who are sanctified (Heb 10:14). He is the one sacrifice, the one mediator (Heb 9:15).

Often our sister Churches in the Western world have accused Roman Catholicism of neglecting this, neglecting the *one sacrifice* by our many Masses, and neglecting the *one mediator* by our saints and our priests. In one way it is not difficult to answer distortions in these objections, but we should not lose the force of what underlies them. In particular, the ordained clergy have not always given priority to the priesthood of Christ over all. To illustrate the problem, I remember a former president of the Lutheran Church in America telling me, "I get many questions from Roman Catholics, and a very common one is, 'Who is the head of your Church?' My answer to them is, 'The head of my Church is the same as the head of your Church, Jesus Christ.' " He is right, but unfortunately we would not always recognize that. In particular, it is not always clear to us that our obedience to Christ must outrank all obedience to human authority. And so, my first point, derived from the priesthood of Christ and looking to the future of priesthood in the Church, concerns how Christians in general, and how ordained priests in particular, will deal with obedience to Jesus Christ in relation to the obedience owed to authority within the Church. That is going to be a really trying issue in the last quarter of this century.

We have sometimes heard, "You are to give blind obedience to church authorities." But can responsible Christians ever give *blind* obedience? In my judgment, the liberty proclaimed by Christ stands against the notion of blind obedience. We are thinking human beings, and no one ever has the right to ask us not to think for ourselves. Religious are sometimes told that their superiors stand in the place of God in the sense that they are vehicles of God's Spirit, and God can be seen active in and through them. I do not question such a principle, but that does not mean that one can give to a human being the obedience owed to God. Precisely because the Holy Spirit is working in and through *human* beings, we are not free to discount the possibility of human distortion when we hear the principle that we are always to do what we are told. People know their priests can be wrong; priests know their bishop can be wrong; and bishops know that Rome can be wrong; and obedience does not excuse the perpetuation of wrong.

Yet we cannot turn the awareness of this into an excuse for adolescent displays of disrespect for church authority, such as we have seen in these last years, when the first reaction to statements of authority has been to send telegrams and place one's protest in the newspaper, forgetting the scriptural injunction first to speak face to face to those with whom you disagree, and then to try to do it in a small group, before calling upon the whole Church (Matt 18:15–17). We must not tear down the kind of loyalty that has made the Church strong, the kind of authority that holds us together in spite of diversity. We cannot call upon obedience to Christ as an excuse for doing what we want in the Church.

How do we bring these two obediences together? Perhaps we have always had this problem, but it is much more urgent in our time. How do we put Christ first and still remain loyal and obedient to those who "are over us in the Lord" (I Thess 5:12), namely, the bishops and, in particular, the Bishop of Rome. And those authorities, commissioned as they are by the whole Church, including the people, to exercise the authority that Christ gave to the Church, how do they keep reminding themselves of the limitations on their exercise of authority? This issue is illustrated by the example of the most exalted human authority in the early Church, Peter, the leader of the Twelve, who was told by Jesus, "Feed *my* lambs. . . . Tend *my* sheep" (John 21:15–17). At the very moment he is described as receiving pastoral authority, he is also taught never to think of the sheep as his own. The sheep belong to Jesus Christ and to him alone; only Jesus can say, "*My* sheep."

In summation, then, of this first point: Vatican II gave all a great sense of responsibility as thinking men and women in the Church of Jesus Christ. I have tried to focus on the problem that will arise from that in terms of our appreciation of the unique priesthood of Jesus Christ, by which he is the sole Head of the Church, the sole mediator.

THE SECOND PRIESTHOOD

A priesthood that gets even more prominence in the NT than the unique high priesthood of Christ is the priesthood of all believers (note, not the unfortunate designation, "the priesthood of the laity," but the priesthood of all believers, shared by laity and clergy alike). We hear from I Peter 2:9, "You are a chosen race, a royal priesthood, a holy nation . . . God's own people," called by God Himself to manifest His wonderful works. I have no doubt that if one were to use the term "priest" in speaking to an audience of first-century Christians, what would be immediately called to mind would be the priesthood of every Christian, of every believing man and woman. It is a priesthood which, as I Peter 2:5 says, manifests itself in "offering spiritual sacrifices acceptable to God"; it is a priesthood of offering sanctified lives through all that we do. In NT times there seems to have been a special stress on offering one's life as a sacrifice for *those who had not yet heard of Christ,* so that they could see in Christian dedication a challenge to believe. I Peter 2:12 goes on to say that Christians are so to live among the Gentiles that they will see the good deeds of the Christians and glorify God. The Book of Revelation (5:9–10) speaks of Christ the lamb: "You did ransom for God men and women from every tribe and tongue and people and nation, and made them a kingdom and priests to our God." And Paul himself, as he writes to the Romans (15:16), speaks of "the grace given me by God to be a minister of Christ Jesus to the Gentiles in priestly service to the Gospel of God." There is no reference here to the eucharist or a priesthood connected with it; rather Paul is thinking of the life that he lives proclaiming the Gospel to the Gentiles, his apostolic form of that priestly life of spiritual dedication to which every Christian is challenged.

Once again, I think that this priesthood of all believers will present a challenge in the Church of our times. In particular, the next 20 years will see a special struggle on the part of ordained priests as they come to grips with the implications of the priesthood of all believers. Vatican II raised the issue but in the only way visible at that time, the role of the faithful in the eucharist. But that is not where the heart of the priesthood of believers lies, even though it includes that. The heart of the believers' priesthood in which we all share is the giving of our whole lives, not just in the eucharist, but in everything that we do. From the moment of our baptism into Christ, our lives constitute a priestly offering to God, and it was probably in the context of Christian baptism that I Peter spoke the words about a royal priesthood, a holy nation and God's own people.

Theoretically, Roman Catholics have always acknowledged this general priesthood; but as I remember hearing of it in theology studies, it was always with a caution: "Remember that there is a metaphysical difference between the ordained priesthood and the priesthood of the faithful, a difference of kind, not just of degree." Yet does not our emphasis have to be in the other direction, not cautionary but encouraging? Do we really need to fear that the distinction will be lost or blurred? Do we rather not need to face the greater problem that most Roman Catholics never think of the priesthood of all believers and are not really able to accept it? After all, in our Church sacred liturgy and life style mark off the ordained priesthood very clearly from the rest of the people of God. (Remember the backwards way in which married laity found their way into the calendar of saints: "neither virgins nor martyrs.") Do we not have to struggle hard to remind ourselves that the priesthood which makes us saints is the priesthood that we all share?

It is claimed that in some ways the shortage of ordained clergy may help this, as by necessity the nonordained are brought in increasing numbers into the public service of the Church, and as believers more visibly exercise their priesthood of dedicated lives. It will be a challenge for ordained priests, many of whom have not been accustomed to think existentially of laity, women and men, as equals, to work side by side with them and occasionally to take instructions from the laity as they function as priests in the Church of Jesus Christ.

The priesthood of believers is illustrated in a special way by Mary. Again, I remember that when I went through the seminary, despite great veneration for Mary, we were always cautioned about calling Mary a priest, because at that time "priest" meant exclusively the sacrificing priest of the eucharist and the implication had to be avoided that Mary offered the eucharist. Holy cards that had her dressed in priestly vestments were avoided as indicative of bad theology (and I agree). Although some Catholic orators would have Mary standing at the foot of the cross gazing upon Jesus and saying, "This is my body," most recognized that as oratorical excess (and again I agree). But the notion of Mary as priest is justifiable biblically in a different way: Every Christian is a priest, and she is the first of Christians. It was she whom Luke 1:38 describes as first to say the words that constitute the basic priestly dedication: "Be it done unto me according to your word." That is the quintessential spirit of the priesthood of all believers. And in the strange system of values that marks the kingdom of God, it is our Catholic belief that when all are evaluated before the divine throne, there will stand first not any of the Twelve, not an apostle, not a pope, not anyone of rank in the hierarchy, not an ordained priest, but a woman. And this woman will rank first not simply because her womb bore the Son of God and her breasts nourished him—that was the praise that the other woman in the crowd wanted to give her (Luke 11:27). But Jesus knew Mary's place better than did the woman in the crowd, and he put his blessing upon Mary because *she heard the word of God and kept it* (Luke 11:28). Until we face the fact that hearing the word of God and living it out is the real source of sanctity in the Church, constituting true rank and privilege and honor, and until we appropriate this in our hearts, we will not understand what the NT teaches us about priesthood. That is the challenge that the Church will have to face in these next years as believing men and women, who have heard their dignity praised in Vatican II, ask how they can exercise that dignity in the service of Christ.

THE THIRD PRIESTHOOD

The Scriptures also mention an ordained priesthood, a priesthood of altar and sacrifice. Such a cultic priesthood, however, is never presented as a Christian institution in the NT (see PB 13–20); rather, we know it in the OT in terms of the Levitical priesthood of Israel, composed of high priest, priests and levites. The whole people of Israel were told, even as later Christians would be told, "You shall be to me a kingdom of priests and a holy nation" (Exod 19:6). Nevertheless, there developed alongside the priesthood of all Israel a specially consecrated priesthood set aside for sacred tasks, one of which was that of offering sacrifices in the name of the people of God. One finds no evidence of a corresponding Christian development in the NT, for no member of the Church is called a priest in relation to the eucharist.

However, a Christian appropriation of the symbolism of the Levitical priesthood does make its appearance in the *First Letter of Clement*, written from the Church of Rome at the very end of the first century, a writing contemporary with the last books of the NT. In chapter 40, Clement says, "He [God] commanded that sacrifices and liturgies be offered, not in a random and irregular fashion, but at fixed times and hours. He has determined, moreover, by His supreme will the places and persons whom He desires for these celebrations. ... Special ministrations are allotted to the high priest; and for the priests a special role has been assigned; and upon the levites their

proper services have been imposed. The lay person is bound by the
rules laid down for the laity."

At this early time in church history, one cannot yet equate Clement's threefold Levitical symbolism with the emerging threefold
Christian pattern of bishop, presbyters and deacons. Recent studies
of Christian worship insist that it was the end of the second century
before the term "priest" began clearly to be applied in a special way
to the Christian minister of the eucharist.[2] And even then in Christian parlance, the eucharistic priesthood does not supplant the priesthood of all believers. Only in the third and fourth centuries can one
begin to take for granted that when "priests" are mentioned the author may well be thinking of the ordained ministers of the eucharist.
However, as we know, this has become the dominant meaning of
priesthood in the Church. Today, when we speak of priests, unless
we explain very carefully, no one is going to think of Jesus Christ,
nor is one going to think of all believers.

In judging this development, once again some of our sister
Churches of the West have accused us of distorting the NT, pointing
out that such a priesthood is not found there, and questioning the
wisdom of an importation from the OT. Personally, I do not think
that one can answer by interpreting the silence of the NT in any other way than that the first Christians had not yet developed the notion
of a cultic priesthood of their own; but I do challenge the notion that
a post-NT development is a distortion. We Catholics should think of
the ordained priesthood as part of our God-given heritage from Israel, which brought into Christian life the wealth and mystery of the
whole area of OT cult. We have managed to preserve, alongside the
uniqueness of the sacrifice and priesthood of Christ, the Levitical
consciousness of the sacred character of a special priestly service that
brings contact with the cultic symbols of God's presence. From this
development has come the expectation that a priest be a person of
signal holiness and even be expected to live a different style of life.

But here again, what has been a strength in Catholicism can
also be a problem. How do we combine such a special priesthood

---

[2]See H.-M. Legrand, "The Presidency of the Eucharist According to the Ancient
Tradition," *Worship* 53 (1979) 413–38.

with the priesthood of all believers? How do we combine the exalted expectations that we have of our ordained priests with the consciousness that as priests they are no less human, and the consciousness of a tremendous demand for sanctity on all Christians? One answer, which was never really approved even in times past, has been subtly to appropriate the sovereignty of the priesthood of Jesus Christ to the priesthood of the ordained, and thus to produce the "prince-priest." Because there were special expectations of the ordained priest, there were also special privileges and special treatment. But the whole ethos of the Church since Vatican II is against special privilege, and the "prince-priest" is doomed. I do not think, however, that the "pal-priest" is much of an improvement, if I may use such a term. This is an appropriation from a sense of the community of all believers: If all are priests, why should anything special by way of holiness or style of life be expected of the ordained priest? And yet, if there is nothing distinctive about the ordained priest, why does he exist? How do ordained priests combine a perception that they are distinct with the perception that they are not better or deserving of privilege? That is perhaps the greatest problem the cultic priesthood faces today.

In answer to this, as I look to the future, I would ask that we return to the influence of the other two priesthoods. There has been a tendency to bring into the ordained priesthood the wrong aspect of the other two priesthoods, to form a "prince-priest" in imitation of the sovereignty of Christ the high priest, or a "pal-priest" in imitation of the commonness of the priesthood of all believers. But let us look at other aspects of those two priesthoods that might strengthen the true distinctiveness of the ordained priesthood.

Although Hebrews insists upon the unique sovereignty of Christ the high priest, it also insists that he did not exalt himself but was appointed by God (5:5); and although he was God's Son, he had to learn obedience through what he suffered (5:8). In the days of his flesh, Christ had to pray and shed tears (5:7) and become able to sympathize with human weaknesses because "He was in every respect tempted as we are, yet without sinning" (4:15). It is not in terms of power and glory but in terms of compassion, suffering, and learning obedience that the ordained priest can imitate Christ the high priest. His eternal sacrifice had meaning because in his life on earth he came to understand what it was to sacrifice himself. So also, the ordained priest's role in the sacrifice of the Mass which makes present again the sacrifice of Jesus Christ makes sense if that priest has learned to sacrifice himself. Such a priesthood has distinctiveness not because it demands privilege but because it helps to exemplify publicly those dispositions that, in the language of Hebrews (5:5), caused Christ to be appointed high priest.

From the priesthood of all believers the ordained priest need not conclude that nothing distinctive can be expected of him by way of life style. Rather, he should conclude that the fundamental demand upon him, too, is that he live out the motto, "Be it done to me according to Your word." Privilege and pomp destroy what the ordained priest shares with all believers. When Christians think of the ordained priesthood, they constantly think of the Last Supper because they relate the service of that priesthood to the words found in Luke's and Paul's account of the eucharist when Jesus said, "Do this in commemoration of me." They often forget that in John's account of the Last Supper there is no eucharist, but in its place there stands the washing of the feet. I never like to read into the mind of the Fourth Evangelist, but I think that his introduction of the washing of the feet had a certain corrective intent. If, by the time he wrote, there was already a deep veneration for the eucharist, there may have already been a sense of privilege associated with it. If many might vie to celebrate the eucharist, not many would really want to wash feet. Yet without that sense of service, a priesthood centered upon the eucharist could become a distortion of what the NT tells us about priesthood. And so, we are fortunate that almost in imitation of Luke's and Paul's word of Jesus at the Last Supper, "Do this in commemoration of me," John (13:14–15) has given us as his form of Jesus' Last Supper command, "If I have washed your feet, you also ought to wash one another's feet. . . . Do as I have done to you." Both are demands of the Master, and the ordained priesthood will not be what it should be without attention to both.

As the Church faces the problem of interrelating its three priesthoods, I foresee struggle in the next twenty years about the role of the ordained priesthood, a struggle both for those already ordained and for those preparing for ordination. Yet, when critically analyzed, the biblical insights about the three priesthoods should enable us in this period that will lead us into the third millennium to put the ordained priesthood in a very positive perspective. Always first for us will be the priesthood of Jesus Christ himself, as we come to appreciate more sensitively that we owe him an obedience owed to no other. We shall come to that millennium as part of a Christian people more conscious than ever of its status as a royal priesthood and a holy nation—priestly and holy in lives offered to God which are valuable in the service of the Church—a people conscious that while an ordained ministry of bishop, priest and deacon is necessary for the functioning of the Church, it does not make the ordained any higher in God's sight than he is already by being a member of the priesthood of all believers through baptism. And yet, we will still be a Catholic people *proud that it continues to call its ministers "priests,"* because their role in the eucharist is distinctive through the example they give by the sacrifice of their lives, and because by their willingness to surrender themselves to God's will they offer a model of the general priesthood that all share.

Chapter Seven
MOVING ALL THE CHURCHES TO REFORM

Summary of the theme:[1] *Biblical studies have played an enormously important role in furthering the ecumenical movement as Protestant and Catholic scholars come to increasing agreement on the literal meaning of the Scriptures. It becomes clear that no Church can claim total fidelity to the Scriptures in details of life, structure, and spirit. While a simple return to the past is not possible, ongoing reform is demanded of the Churches in the light of Christ's ideals and those of the early Christians—different reforms are required of Roman Catholicism and of Protestantism.*

Much of what has been said thus far concerns the impact of biblical criticism on Christians in the Church. In these last two chapters let me turn to the further impact on ecumenical relations among the Churches. From my remarks at the end of the last chapter the reader may surmise that I am one of the many who think almost mystically about entering another millennium of world history.

---

[1]The material represented in this chapter was originally delivered in the Miller Chapel of the Princeton Theological Seminary on November 13, 1979 at a service commemorating the fifteenth anniversary of the promulgation of the Vatican II Decree on Ecumenism (*Unitatis redintegratio*) on November 21,1964. It has not been previously published.

For the Churches January 1, 2000 might well be looked on as a day of judgment, if between now and then they make no significant movement toward reunifying Christianity. A lack of progress would mean that Christianity will enter the third millennium badly divided, whereas it entered the second millennium relatively united. One thousand years will have been completed in which Christians increasingly disregarded their Master's will that they be one (John 17:20–21). On January 1, 1000 there had as yet been no affirmed schism rending Christianity into Eastern Orthodoxy and Roman Catholicism; there had been no splintering of the Western Church into a hundred quarreling denominations. A Christianity that has now become accustomed to division as an ordinary way of life should call itself to judgment as to whether it cannot undo some of the harm, before it enters the third thousand years of proclaiming a Lord who said, "This is my commandment: Love one another as I have loved you" (John 15:12).

It may help us to reflect that chronologically we stand between the calling of Vatican Council II by Pope John XXIII in January 1959 and the millennium point in January 2000. Pope John made a tremendous shift in Roman policy toward ecumenism when he insisted on inviting "the faithful of the separated communities" to the Council. If we look to the ecumenical changes and growth in the two decades since the Council, we may have a better idea of what is possible in the decades remaining before this century closes.

As below I discuss both past and future changes, I am aware that sometimes I am ranging beyond the direct effects of modern *biblical* study. Nevertheless, one should not underplay the influence of biblical criticism in efforts to reform the Churches. The Protestant Reformation of the sixteenth century was generated by an appeal to the Bible, as theologians looked at the Church of their time and realized how different it had become from what was described in the NT. In a much gentler way the self-reform of Roman Catholicism in the twentieth century came from the same roots. As we saw in Chapter Four, the biblical movement was farther along than almost any other Catholic intellectual ferment at the time of Vatican II; and minds honed to explore the tensions between the literal meaning of the Scriptures and Church interpretation (as described in Chapter Two) will always be prodding the Churches to *metanoia* or change of outlook. Thus, I would argue that a modern view of the Bible has, at least indirectly, contributed much to what I am about to describe.

ECUMENICAL CHANGES SINCE VATICAN II

In 1954 at the Evanston (Ill.) Assembly of the World Council of Churches, the Argentinian Methodist, Santos Barbieri, delivered a stirring attack on the faults of Roman Catholicism; he was subsequently elected to the presidency of the World Council because of his contributions to ecumenism. At the same time, Cardinal Stritch warned Catholics against attending the Evanston meeting.[2] It was a remarkable reversal, then, when five years after Vatican II, by agreement between Rome and Geneva, I became one of the dozen or so Roman Catholic members of the Faith and Order Commission of the World Council, so that Catholics are now able to contribute to the theological thinking of that ecumenical body. In this short time we have moved from prohibiting attendance to active participation!

But one does not have to go to Evanston to document twenty years of change; one might do that at theological schools. In mid-century, when Catholics were still forbidden to read Protestant books critical of the Catholic Church or its doctrine, the idea of a Catholic on a Protestant theology faculty would have been actively resisted. Today Roman Catholics teach on the most prestigious faculties, and many Catholic seminaries have Protestant faculty members in key spots. Protestant students who have learned from Roman Catholic scholars as teachers and authors can scarcely preach hostility against Catholics or generalize so easily about the Church; and Catholic students who have learned from Protestant scholars cannot share the attitude of the older textbooks which took notice of Protestants chiefly in terms of adversaries to be refuted. In the field of Bible, many American Catholic scholars would scarcely have been known to Protestant scholars twenty years ago; today they are among the top contributors in the biblical guild. As late as the 1930s it was still discouraged by the Roman Catholic Church that its scholars belong to national and international biblical societies of

---

[2]For these details see G. H. Tavard, *Two Centuries of Ecumenism* (New York: Mentor-Omega, 1962) 146.

Protestant and Jewish scholars. Today numerous Catholics have served as presidents of such organizations. Catholic and Protestant scholars have worked together to produce studies of common agreement on such ecumenically sensitive topics as the roles of Peter and of Mary in the NT.[3]

Even if we confine ourselves to the direct ecumenical results of Vatican Council II, they are impressive. A reconciliation between East and West has been symbolized as the Bishop of Rome met both the Ecumenical (Orthodox) Patriarch and the Coptic Patriarch. This has been accompanied by the cancellation of ancient anathemas and the return of patronal relics to Orthodox sees. Such gestures may seem quaint to us, but they remove offenses that have been like thorns beneath the skin since the time of the crusades. On a local level the presence of the church leaders of one group at the installation or ordination of the church leaders of another group is a sign of warmth and friendship. Union may not yet be achieved, but there is brotherhood. More practically, the Roman Catholic Church, the largest of the Christian bodies, has moved from adamant opposition to ecumenism to pouring much energy and time into the movement. The very existence of the Vatican Secretariat for Christian Unity shows that. The ongoing bilateral dialogues between the Roman Catholic Church and individual other Churches have removed past bitterness and made real contributions to theology, especially of the eucharist and of ministry. We have begun to see that theologically and biblically ecumenical studies are not an option or a luxury but a necessity.

Some observers lament how slow the ecumenical movement is, how far we have to go, how many areas have yet to see results. While all of that is true, it is worth noting in terms of Roman Catholic relationships to other Churches, that there has been more progress in the last twenty years than in the whole 450 years since the Augsburg Confession (1530). But, you may wonder, are we not at a standstill now in terms of movement toward the organic union of Churches? One can speak of Catholic members in Faith and Order, but the Ro-

---

[3]*Peter in the New Testament,* ed. R. E. Brown *et al.* (New York: Paulist, & Minneapolis: Augsburg, 1973); *Mary in the New Testament,* ed. R. E. Brown *et al.* (New York: Paulist, & Philadelphia: Fortress, 1978).

man Catholic Church is not moving toward membership in the World Council. Even if one takes note of impressive statements from the bilateral dialogues, Rome has never officially confirmed such agreements. In part, such slowness derives from the Roman Catholic Church situation of the last few years. In his final years, as his health was failing, Pope Paul VI clearly decided against major actions that would bind his successor. The rapid succession of the two Popes John Paul complicated what might have been a smoother replacement. True, John Paul II has now been pope for some time; but much of his energy has gone to consolidating his own position, becoming familiar as an outsider with Rome, and as an Eastern European with the Church at large. Ecumenism has not been "on the front burner," and so it remains to be seen what will happen.[4] Nor, as a matter of fact, has ecumenism been as much in the forefront in the programs of some of the major Protestant Churches. Declining membership, financial problems, and inner disputes have caused Protestants to be more inward looking than was true in the 1960s and early 1970s.

*   *   *

But rather than speculate on what church leaders will do in the next twenty years, I would like to concentrate on the spirit of reform necessary if we are to grow together to the point of organic union. And now I begin to concentrate on the relationship between Roman Catholicism and the classic Churches descended from the Protestant Reformation. I do not mean to slight the free Churches or the Churches that grew up on the North American continent; in the U.S.A. they probably outnumber Christians descended from the Lutheran and Calvinist Reforms and from the Church of England. But, practically, Rome's first steps toward union with Protestants will involve the historic Churches it has known in Europe for centuries. If healing occurs in that area, further healing relations with the outer perimeters of the Reformation may become more possible. Even if we confine ourselves to the classic Churches, however, it must be

---

[4]Pope John Paul's visit to Germany in late 1980, after some initial awkwardness, contained important gestures in support of Lutheran/Catholic relations.

recognized that numerically Rome is not an equal partner in dialogue. Its massive constituency all over the world makes a Catholic-
Lutheran dialogue or a Catholic-Anglican dialogue somewhat
lopsided. I mention size because there is a problem as to how reform
can affect the large and varied Roman Catholic Church.

In my early days in professional biblical work I reviewed somewhat sharply a book by Professor J. K. S. Reid of Edinburgh[5] in
which he referred to the Roman Catholic Church as the *unreformed*
Church. Before I read that description, existentially I had not realized that in the eyes of many Protestants the largest branch of Christianity had never been reformed, despite the Council of Trent. Such
an attitude is probably far less frequent among reflective Protestants
today precisely because of the self-reformation steps taken at Vatican
Council II. (I spent some time with Professor Reid in August 1979 at
a Faith and Order subcommission meeting in Geneva, and in the
face of his kindness it was rather embarrassing to remember my bris-
tling reaction of so long ago.) The Catholic attitude toward the Reformation of the sixteenth century may be changing in a
corresponding manner. More Catholics realize today that the classi-
cal Reformers for the most part did not intend to found separate
Churches but to call the large Church back to being what it should
be in terms of preaching the Gospel. Even if Roman Catholics may
not agree with the Reformers' vision of what the Church should be,
the religious zeal of a Luther and Calvin and the need for a reformation in the Roman Church of those times can be appreciated, especially since the Lateran Council V had been called in 1512–17 for
that very purpose but failed. But it remains a delicate point whether
Roman Catholics can ever say it was a good thing that the sixteenth-
century Reformation did occur. Protestants have a Reformation
Sunday, and frequently Roman Catholics are asked to participate so
that it will be clear that the celebration has a positive tone and is not
meant as anti-Catholic. But even when they participate, Roman
Catholics continue to wonder whether the reforms could not have
been brought about without a division of the Church, and whether

---

[5] *The Authority of Scripture* (London: Methuen, 1957), reviewed in TS 19 (1958)
413–15.

the fact that the Lutheran and Calvinist Reforms produced bitter hostility did not make it more difficult for Roman Catholicism to engage in necessary self-reform. Nevertheless, the Reformation released a spirit of free and critical thinking that probably was not possible from within Roman Catholicism. For instance, one has to wonder whether modern historical criticism both in theology and biblical work could ever have arisen within Roman Catholicism. And so even Catholics who cannot bring themselves to agree that the Reformation was either inevitable or laudable have to admit that considerable good came as it was lived out by sincere Christians.

One way of looking at Vatican Council II is in terms of the reform which was not done *from within* in the sixteenth century. Gone now are the German princes, the Holy Roman Emperor, and the proud and nationalistic English king—complicating factors that turned the earlier movement to reform the Church into a movement that produced separate Churches. In the twentieth century a large, tranquil, prosperous Church, which was not under fire from the outside, asked itself about reforms that needed to be made in order to be more Christian and to preach the Gospel more effectively in the world. Almost all the previous councils that Roman Catholics call ecumenical had been assembled because of dangers from the outside, especially heresies. But this council was for self-examination at a time when there was no danger of heresy. Inevitably such self-examination has produced turmoil in the Church, to the point where some Catholics now wish that there had never been a Vatican Council II, because in their minds Catholicism was a better and more observant religion before the Council. I suppose that if undisturbed uniformity is the norm, Roman Catholicism did a foolish thing at Vatican II. But tranquility may stem from a failure to examine difficulties, and uniformity may come from a suppression of differences. Jesus of Nazareth did not place value on undisturbed uniformity; he placed enormous emphasis on reform of life and way of thinking (*metanoia*). As I emphasized at the end of Chapter Five he was a disturbing figure who probed the established religion of his time with many questions; and if one judges Christianity in the light of the probing Jesus, then Roman Catholicism did what it should have done at Vatican II.

ONGOING ROMAN CATHOLIC REFORM

If Vatican Council II may be looked upon as an inner Roman Catholic reformation, I wish to ask whether in these next twenty years a continuation may not produce what Christians on all sides might wish to achieve: a truly reformed Catholic Church. This Church, with a distinctive Roman component to be sure, might heal the divisions of Christianity. Such a vision of the Catholic Church places a demand on both Roman Catholics and Protestants for continued reform. And so I wish to challenge not only my own ecclesiastical communion but also other Christian communions.

Let me turn for a moment to the experience of the most famous Protestant theologian of this century, Karl Barth. Recently I read a description of the last days of his life. He had developed the habit of listening to radio sermons (which we may hope are more substantial in Switzerland than those we hear). On December 8th, 1968, the feast of the Immaculate Conception of Mary, he heard on that topic a Roman Catholic sermon which intrigued him. At the same time he himself was writing a sermon to be given in January in the week set aside for prayer for Christian unity. This sermon, planned for Zurich at the invitation of Roman Catholics working together with a reformed group, was entitled, "Starting Out, Turning Around, and Confessing." One can ponder what Barth meant by those terms, but I imagine that "reformation" might be a good one-word description of the implications of starting out, turning around, and confessing. Somewhere in the night following December 9th, one day later, Karl Barth died, leaving the sermon in the middle of a sentence, unfinished. It was in this sermon, which contained the last words Barth ever wrote, that he suggested: "The movement of the church starting out, turning around, and confessing . . . is surprisingly more visible, and even spectacular, in the Petrine than in the evangelical confession."[6] Earlier in life Barth had changed the direction of Protestant thought by challenging the liberalism prevalent in European university faculties and thus turning the scientific study of theology back to the service of the Church. And here he was once again at the end of his life issuing a challenge to Protestantism, wondering whether, if I

---

[6]*Final Testimonies* (Grand Rapids: Eerdmans, 1977) 54.

may use the term, reformation was now not more active in the Roman Church than in the Protestant Churches. I want to develop that question in terms of the next twenty years.

Roman Catholicism has made a tremendous start toward self-reform, and the machinery and forces are there to continue it. I recognize that this ongoing reform is not going to be smooth, but many minds and hearts and energies in the Roman Catholic Church are now totally directed to issues that were also matters of concern in the sixteenth-century Reformation. I think, for instance, about a continued reform of the liturgy so that it becomes a binding force in the Christian community, about preaching the Scriptures, and about worship in the people's own language. The startling changes in these areas in Roman Catholicism will go on; and the realization that this is crucial may be seen from the way we debate, sometimes acrimoniously, every liturgical practice. Not all new liturgical experiments have been good; but behind them is a burning ambition that the liturgy be a true service, rendering glory to God and giving instruction and encouragement to the people. Many Protestants would recognize that in these last years Roman Catholicism has led the way in showing Christians what liturgy should be, a leadership visible in such features as a revamped lectionary with a wider variety of passages from the Scriptures, and a more visible union between the preaching elements and the eucharistic elements.

Another area of Catholic self-reform, echoing the interests of the Protestant Reformation, has been that of a greater participation of the Christian people in church life and thought. One facet of this is the diversity within Roman Catholic practice. We are an international Church that is just learning to profit from the enriching diversity of its membership. In a sense previous uniformity, although it made things easier, suppressed what the various people of the world could contribute to Catholic Christianity. I am not an enthusiast for liberation theology, but it is startling that from the Third World countries of Latin America comes a major theological movement that could not have been anticipated in a more uniform Church where Roman Universities set the standards for theology. Suddenly countries, once considered as theological (and economic) backwaters, have begun to make a contribution stemming from their own experience of proclaiming the Gospel in difficult circumstances.

However locally conditioned their thought, the rest of the Church has had to listen. Forces have been unleashed that are making the Roman Catholic Church learn "from below," and not *exclusively* from the hierarchy. At times, fear may slow this process down, but the basic dynamism is irreversible.

Parenthetically, let me remark that in my judgment many Catholics have misread the import of the changes introduced. When one states that there is now a synod of elected bishops to advise the pope, and a senate of elected priests to advise the bishop, and a parish council to advise the pastor, a cynical response is often evoked: These are only advisory, and decisive power remains in the hands of one man. I think that is a misreading of the signs. Once such consultative bodies have been introduced, eventually they have an effect. No human relationship is possible if the person who makes the decision consistently vetoes the advice of the group he consults. No matter how inclined to resist, eventually authority will go along with the majority on many issues; for that is part of the dynamism of the consultative system. Obviously this development will take some time, but why must we Catholics be so impatient, so that if changes are not evident immediately, we assume they will never come? (In all this, as any intelligent American or Englishman knows, democracy is not a perfect system. Indeed, one may arouse antagonism when one speaks of ecclesiastical democracy because of the debatable theology that the Roman Catholic Church is a monarchy.[7] But under whatever name, there is value on every level in having a wide input from people as the Church makes decisions.) I would insist that a collegial force is at work, and the machinery for consultation is in place; eventually they will broaden the decision-making process.

Another area of self-reform which is related to the implications of the sixteenth-century Reformation involves the relationship between the Roman Catholic magisterium and Catholic theologians—a relationship, already discussed in Chapter Three, that affects freedom of thought. In some instances this relationship is still somewhat uneasy, as attested by the Küng and Schillebeeckx cases. Roman au-

---

[7]The Kingdom of God is a divine monarchy, but the Church cannot simply be identified with Kingdom of God. Acceptance of the pope's role and authority need not make him a king.

thorities may need to reflect on whether such procedures do not do more damage than good, for the combination of Catholics and Protestants scandalized by the action against Küng would surely outnumber the relatively few Catholics scandalized by reading Küng. (More numerous are Catholics who proclaim themselves scandalized by Küng without ever having read for themselves a word he wrote— a group of hearsay vigilantes who should be ignored simply for justice' sake.) Nevertheless, those cases are an exception, as we have seen; and theologians now have much more freedom and voice than before Vatican II. This is apparent if one reflects on the repressive attitude toward theologians in the Roman anti-Modernist purges, especially in the 1920s. Not only were certain Bible professors forbidden to teach (although they held views that now would be considered quite conservative), but so were all those who had studied under them. Such prohibitions created a fear of innovative writing among Catholic scholars. Even as late as thirty years ago the idea was voiced authoritatively that the function of the theologian was to supply arguments for the decisions of the magisterium.[8] This constricted view is simply not current anymore. Even if there are sometimes strains between the official teachers of the Church (the magisterium) and those who investigate and teach theology, the Church now expresses itself as grateful to theologians for their original contributions.[9] It cannot treat them simply as servants of the magisterium. ("Servants of the Church" has a positive sense, but the Church is wider than the magisterium.) What has developed is a form of working partnership, not an absolute dominance. I would hope that from the Protestant experience one may learn that a Church dominated by theologians would not be good, and no serious Catholic theologian would wish that. The issue is one of establishing a constructive relationship between the need to investigate new questions honestly (sometimes with shocking implications, at least upon initial impact) and the pastoral care for the faithful. Undoubtedly there will be awkward moments in establishing the right balance and probably an occasional future condemnation of a theologian, but the dynamism for

[8] See Pope Pius XII, *Humani generis* (DBS 3886).
[9] See the remarks of Pope John Paul II in the dedication of this book.

responsible freedom is now present in the Roman Catholic Church. There is no possibility of reverting to a pre-Vatican II situation.

In another area of self-reform since Vatican II pertinent to Protestant interests, there is less Catholic dependence on law. In my view law is unobjectionable in itself; but a Christian problem arises when a Church begins to do all the thinking for its people through law. The relaxation of many laws since Vatican II has meant that there is much more individual thinking among Roman Catholics today, even where laws continue to exist. Precisely because this has been an *internal* reform, disagreement of the faithful with church authority has not produced much hostility. In the 1979 visit of Pope John Paul II to the U.S.A., many Catholics enthusiastically applauded him even though they were in practical disagreement with a few of his ethical stances, e.g., on artificial birth control. This seeming contradiction puzzled many commentators; but it was an instance of respect for authority combined with an independent following of conscience— surely not something ideal in its conflicts, but a fact in Roman Catholic life. Many of the faithful sympathize with someone who has to speak for and command the larger Church, even if in their own lives they cannot fully appropriate that command. The pope and bishops, while not ceasing to proclaim what they regard as gospel demands, seem pastorally tolerant toward such inability. Some Roman Catholics have been embittered by the tension; but sympathy, not hostility, is characteristic of many more. In any case, self-responsibility has entered the picture on a large scale, and there is every prospect that it will continue.

NEED FOR PROTESTANT REFORM

I have spoken of the prospect of continued self-reform in the Roman Catholic Church. Now what about the Protestant Churches? Let me ask some pointed questions; for sometimes I get the feeling that many Protestants are saying smugly, "Well finally Rome is reforming, and perhaps one day it will reach where we are." To my mind such an attitude would be a sign that the Protestant Churches are no longer heirs of the Reformation, because real reform is a continuing process. Reform should be as much a challenge to Protestants as to Roman Catholics, even if sometimes the latter have been said to belong to "the unreformed Church." Looking forward to the coming years, we need to know whether there is a real reforming activity in process in the classic Protestant Churches. Is there the thrust and the machinery for continuing self-reform that might bring Christianity together before the year 2000? Even if Rome continues to reform itself, unity will not result unless Protestants reform themselves, so that our paths converge. I ask the following questions in friendship and not with hidden antagonism. My own experience of teaching for a decade in Union Theological Seminary (N.Y.C.) has given me a concern for the future of Protestantism. And precisely because I have asked these questions of my Church, I feel free to ask them of other Churches as well.

I grow fearful that some Protestants have forgotten a basic concern of the Reformation, namely, the Gospel rightly preached. Today, with the inroads of secularism, are basic Gospel questions asked any more from some Protestant pulpits, for instance, questions about Christ? Or is there simply a litany of social concerns? I am not talking now about the conservative Bible Churches but the mainline Protestant Churches. In Roman Catholicism one can still get a fight over the reality of Jesus' resurrection, over his virginal conception, over the christological statements of Chalcedon. Some may scoff that that is because we are a retrograde Church; but I think it is because we still recognize that christological issues are basic to the very nature of Christianity and the Gospel. When I read the frequent Protestant statements of concern about social issues, I see a danger. Many preachers may convince themselves that, when they are speaking against racial prejudice in South Africa, they are preaching the Gospel. However, attacking the South African situation before a liberal congregation might ensure the preacher that no parishioner will be angry with him, but preaching to such a congregation about the divinity of Jesus Christ might provoke embarrassment and offense. If preaching the Gospel means mentioning the unmentionable, then the christological message is often what would disturb liberal congregations.

One may make the same point on issues of sexual morality. The Roman magisterium speaks so frequently on marriage, sex, birth control, and abortion that church leaders are subject to the accusation that as celibates they are "hung up on sex." But have not many mainline Protestant Churches gone to the opposite extreme? Has it not become unfashionable among many to say anything corrective about sexual morals? I am sadly amused to find every disapproving attitude dismissed as "victorian." If one reads the NT, it soon becomes clear that Queen Victoria is being given the credit for concerns that were apostolic and Pauline. A glance at I Corinthians should illustrate the fact that the sex and marriage problems have been legitimate matters of concern for church authorities from the beginning. Preaching the Gospel has to bring the demand of Jesus to bear on that area where most human beings struggle with the proper relationships between their own pleasure and their obligations to others, such as spouse and children. Once again, many times it is far easier to speak publicly on social questions that have won common consent, and to leave individuals to work out entirely for themselves what God might want of them in their personal lives. I have no sympathy for a Church that "butts into" everything, but no sympathy either for a Church that is afraid to say anything about sex.

Already John Paul II has been labeled as ultra-conservative (usually by those who have no idea how wild Catholic ultra-conservatives really are). But whether or not one agrees with his every position, he is doing what his people expect when he speaks on matters christological in relation to Küng, or on matters of sex and marriage to the people of every country that he visits. Luther and Calvin might understand far better John Paul II's sense of what is involved in preaching the Gospel than what passes for Gospel in some of the liberal pulpits of churches descended from their Reformation. And if rightly administering the sacraments is part of the Protestant confessional understanding of what the Church is all about, the sixteenth-century reformers might have some very harsh things to say to their descendants—not only about the infrequency of the eucharist, but also about a lack of a sacramental understanding of Christianity, so that the holiness of the Church and the divine orientation of worship is neglected.

This moves us to the whole question of the importance given to "Church" in mainline Protestantism. Roman Catholicism has manifested great diversity since Vatican II, even to the point of extremes. There are liberal Catholics who would change everything and right-wing Catholics who think too much has been changed. The other morning a woman came in after Mass to tell me that it was wrong for Vatican Council II to have made a liturgical change from the Tridentine Mass; for, she proclaimed, "The Church of Christ cannot change." Rather, I would answer, Christ cannot change; but the Church of Christ, which consists of human beings, can and must change. Nevertheless, with all the awkwardness we have had with our extremes (and some would cite the example of Archbishop Lefebvre on one side, and of Küng on the other), there has been no major split from the Roman Church. There remains in Roman Catholicism a sense of the heinousness of church division, so that leaving the Church is the ultimate offense. While theologically they may think very differently, when Lefebvre and Küng say Mass, both mention Pope John Paul II in the eucharistic canon. No matter how much they may dislike him, they would have a sense that not to mention the pope in the canon would be a sign that one is no longer a *Roman* Catholic. I said above that Luther and Calvin desired not to establish new Churches but only to reform the one true Church. Yet has that sense of the oneness of the Church survived in practice in the mainline Churches descended from the Protestant Reformation? In the U.S.A. in the last ten years has there not occurred still another division in the Lutheran, Presbyterian, and Anglican Churches, so that new splinter Churches have been formed? The tendency to divide again and again, so evident in the early period of the Reformation, seems still to be at work. The freedom to form a splinter Church should not be praised as the freedom of the Gospel. Dividing the Church is an offense to the Gospel, and the purpose of true reform is to heal our divisions in loyalty to the Gospel.

I would like to ask, too, about the relationship of the mainline Protestant Churches to theological scholarship. Let me leave aside the instance of conservative Protestant Churches who make headlines from time to time by purging their seminaries of professors who do not uphold the literal inerrancy of the Bible. I have already spoken of Roman Catholic abuses of church authority earlier in this century, and so I know that both sides have their conservative extremists. What I have in mind now is the seeming indifference of the authorities of the liberal Protestant Churches to what their theologians say. Sometimes that is invoked as an instance of freedom of thought. But while I have argued above that the self-reform of Roman Catholicism may require greater freedom of theological investigation, I would judge that part of Protestant self-reform would be a greater concern about theology. I would rather live in a Church whose authorities can get excited and worried over what theologians are saying, even to the point of chastising them, than in a Church that ignores them. Theologians still have the power to nettle the authorities of the Roman Catholic Church and make them think; Protestant theologians are often completely irrelevant to the policy-makers of their Churches, so that the Churches cannot be reformed any more by theological insight. The average Catholic scholar, in my opinion, would rather have the feeling that "somebody up there" in the magisterium is watching, even if occasionally that creates an uncomfortable tension, than deal with the church authorities who could not care less. Indifference may be a crueler fate than correction.

Despite my desire to serve as a friend by asking these uncomfortable questions of the Protestantism I have encountered, I remain an outsider; and true reform comes from within. Roman Catholicism is currently full of people who are asking questions of the Church; my hope would be to see a similar movement within Protestantism (and not only on social questions). Churches founded by reformers should still be capable of producing theological reformers! The most probing questions will come from those who know the strength of their Protestant Churches and can work with love and sympathy to make them even more what they should be.

*   *   *

As helpful as bilateral dialogues have been, ultimately they cannot produce church unity. Councils of Churches make an important contribution, but they cannot heal the heart of the division. Churches that reform themselves from within will ultimately find a great deal in common with other Churches who are disturbed over their present situation and are changing themselves in loyalty to the Gospel. Karl Barth was asking the right question on the night in which he died when he wondered where one could find best expressed that never ending process of starting out, turning around, and confessing. If the Churches spend a good deal of time worrying about that question in the next twenty years, we may cross to the year 2000 as part of a Christianity that is more united than it has been for the last 1000 years.

Chapter Eight
AN EXAMPLE:
RETHINKING THE EPISCOPATE
OF THE NT CHURCHES

Summary of the theme:[1] *Part of the scriptural invitation to ecumenical reform involves a review of Christian origins, since often the Churches have justified their present institutions by an appeal to the past, not realizing that in preserving some values, they have lost others. A modern study of NT episcopate and governance casts new light on many arguments used in the Reformation disputes, arguments now seen to have been overly simplified.*

W e have discussed some general implications for ecumenism that flow from the NT critically read, so that the challenge of early church ideals is presented sharply to the divided Christianity of

---

[1]The material presented in this chapter was originally published in TS 41 (1980) 322–38 under the title: "*Episkopē* and *Episkopos:* The New Testament Evidence"; also in *Episkopé and Episcopate in Ecumenical Perspective* (Faith and Order Paper 102; Geneva: World Council of Churches, 1980) 15–29. Let me emphasize that this is a brief NT survey. If others think of items I have not mentioned, I respond only that I have listed all that I could find of importance. There is no attempt to supply in the footnotes a bibliography on episcopal ministry; one may consult A. Lemaire, *Les ministères aux origines de l'église* (LD 68; Paris: Cerf, 1971); *Le ministère et les ministères selon le Nouveau Testament,* ed. J. Delorme (Paris: Seuil, 1974); B. Cooke, *Ministry to Word and Sacraments* (Philadelphia: Fortress, 1976). Also PB 47–86 for a consecutive history.

our time. But now let me turn to a specific problem of church structure. Christianity is very divided over whether a bishop (Greek *episkopos*) should be the chief pastoral officer of a Church. In the past
the argument has centered on whether or not the episcopal office is
clearly mandated in the NT, or even is of divine institution in the
sense that Jesus foresaw and clearly willed it (pp. 76–78 above). Today those who opt for divine institution might understand that more
subtly as the guidance of the Spirit leading some Churches in the
first century to develop a bishopric—a development so helpful for
unifying the Churches that it became universal in the second and
third centuries. I do not pretend that biblical criticism can resolve
the division on this point among contemporary Churches, but a
study of the evidence can help us to understand that the NT situation was more complicated than our sixteenth-century forebears on
either side thought.

While Catholics know the term *episkopos* ("supervisor, bishop")
very well, the attention given recently to the term *episkopē* ("supervision") may be puzzling. It appears chiefly in ecumenical discussions
as Christians seek to verbalize the fact that most Churches have fixed
lines of authority and supervision, but only some Churches have
bishops. Thus, when an episcopally structured Church considers
union with a nonepiscopally structured Church, another question
should precede the obvious question about the attitude toward having supervision in the hands of one called an *episkopos*. The first
question involves detecting elements of *episkopē*, i.e., supervision in
matters pastoral, doctrinal, and sacramental. It is necessary to realize that there can be *episkopē* without an *episkopos*, and that even in
episcopally structured Churches not all *episkopē* is in the hands of
the *episkopoi*. Because the NT is quite instructive on this score, I
have been called upon for information in several recent ecumenical
enterprises. I took part in the background discussions preparatory to
the report by the U.S. Bishops' Committee on Ecumenical and Inter-
religious Affairs made to the National Council of Catholic Bishops
on "Bilateral Discussions concerning Ministry."[2] We find there:

---

[2]Published in *Interface* (Spring 1979, no. 1) with the horrendous misprint on p. 3:
". . . that the term [apostle] is now always to be equated with the Twelve." Read "not"
for "now."

"Episkopé (i.e., pastoral overseeing of a community) in the New Testament is exercised in different ways by persons bearing different names." More recently the Faith and Order Commission of the World Council of Churches, which is involved in revising its extremely important collection of Agreed Statements on "One Baptism, One Eucharist, and a Mutually Recognized Ministry," recognized the need to amplify the treatment of episcopacy found in the ministry section of the document. I was asked as a member of the Faith and Order Commission to do a *summary* of the NT evidence on the subject.

There are several ways to approach this issue. If one considers the Greek vocabularly most directly expressing the idea of supervision in the NT,[3] it is obvious that those called *episkopoi* exercised some form of *episkopē,* but so did others. Therefore I have thought it best to begin by tracing supervision by other types of people in NT times, and then finally to come to those who were called supervisors. In the NT only the Pastoral Epistles are *ex professo* concerned with church structure, and undoubtedly there was more supervision and supervisory structure than we know about. Since second-century institutions and church officers were not a *creatio ex nihilo,* studies of the post-NT period must also be made as complements to and continuations of NT studies. However, it would be extremely dangerous to assume that the second-century structures which are never mentioned in the NT already existed in the first century. We must allow for the possibility of development and of increasing structuralization as the great figures of the early period became distant memories, and local Churches had to survive on their own.

THE TWELVE

In Acts 1:20, Luke has Peter citing Ps 109(108):8: "His *episkopē* let another take," in reference to replacing Judas as a member of the Twelve. This means that, as Luke looked back on the early

---

[3]The total NT occurrences of three pertinent NT words are as follows: *episkopein,* "to supervise, oversee, inspect, care for," I Pet 5:2; plus Heb 12:15, which is not directly relevant to our quest; *episkopē,* "position of supervisor, function of supervising, visit, visitation," Acts 1:20; I Tim 3:1, plus the not directly relevant passages in Luke

Church from his position ca. A.D. 80, the members of the Twelve were thought to have had a function of supervising. What did that consist in?

All the Gospels portray a group of the Twelve existing during Jesus' ministry, and I Cor 15:5 implies that they were in existence by the time of the resurrection appearances. Therefore there is little reason to doubt that Jesus chose the Twelve. Why did he do this? We have only one saying attributed to Jesus himself about the purpose of the Twelve: he had chosen them to sit on (twelve) thrones judging the twelve tribes of Israel (Matt 19:28; Luke 22:28–30).[4] Seemingly the idea was that in the renewed Israel which Jesus was proclaiming there were to be twelve men, just as there were twelve sons of Jacob/ Israel at the beginnings of the original Israel. The Dead Sea Scrolls community of the New Covenant adopted the same symbolism, for they had a special group of twelve in their Community Council (IQS 8:1).

Besides the role attributed to the Twelve by Jesus himself, the

---

19:44; I Pet 2:12; *episkopos,* "supervisor, overseer, superintendent, bishop," Acts 20:28; Philip 1:1; I Tim 3:2; Titus 1:7; I Pet 2:25.

[4]In the 1976 Declaration "On the Question of the Admission of Women to the Ministerial Priesthood" by the Sacred Congregation for the Doctrine of the Faith (USCC publication, p. 25) there is a most curious passage. In discussing "the attitude of Christ," the Declaration discounts the force of this saying of Jesus for several reasons: (1) Its symbolism is not mentioned by Mark and John. Since when is the antiquity of "Q" material called into question by its absence in Mark (since that is by definition the nature of "Q" material) or *mirabile dictu* by its absence in John? (2) It does not appear in the context of the call of the Twelve, but "at a relatively late stage of Jesus' public life." However, it has been a commonplace in scholarship, explicitly recognized in the 1964 Instruction of the Pontifical Biblical Commission on "The Historical Truth of the Gospels," that the Gospel material is not arranged in historical order (BRCFC 114); and so late occurrence of a statement in the existing order of Matthew and Luke tells us *absolutely nothing* about the attitude of Jesus or when he said it in relation to the Twelve. (3) The essential meaning of the choosing of the Twelve is to be found in the words of Mark 3:14: "He appointed Twelve; they were to be his companions and to be sent out to preach." These words (which are words of Mark and not of Jesus) tell us how Mark understood the role of the Twelve; they most certainly may not be used to overrule the words of Jesus himself in determining "the attitude of Christ" toward the Twelve! Fortunately it is a firm principle in theology that loyal acceptance of a Roman document does not require that one approve the reasons offered.

Evangelists describe them as being given a missionary task, e.g., "to be sent out to preach and to have authority over demons" (Mark 3:14–15; 6:7).[5] In particular, during the ministry of Jesus Matt 10:5–6 has the Twelve being sent to the lost sheep of the house of Israel, and after the resurrection Matt 28:16–20 has them (minus Judas) being told to go and make disciples of all nations, baptizing them and teaching them. Nevertheless, we do not know that in fact all or most of them did this, since all the references to the Twelve as a group after the ministry of Jesus portray them in Jerusalem. Indeed, one gets the impression that little was known of most of them as individuals, and by the last third of the century the names of some of them were being confused and forgotten.[6] Only the first four in all the lists of the Twelve, the two sets of brothers, Peter and Andrew, James and John, have any significant role in the NT. With or without Andrew they are portrayed as having a special role in the ministry of Jesus (Mark 1:16–20; 5:37; 9:2; 13:3; 14:33). In Acts 3:1; 4:13; 8:14, Peter and John play a prominent role in early preaching; and Gal 2:9 shows Peter (Cephas) and John at Jerusalem in the year 49. James of Zebedee, the brother of John, died a martyr's death in the early 40s (Acts 12:2). The only one of the Twelve ever pictured outside Palestine in the NT is Peter, who went to Antioch (Gal 2:11) and perhaps to Corinth (I Cor 1:12; 9:5). Otherwise the NT is silent on the fate of the members of the Twelve. The image of them as carrying on missionary endeavors all over the world has no support in the NT or in other reliable historical sources. The archeological and later documentary evidence that Peter died at Rome is credible; but the rest of the Twelve could have died in Jerusalem, so far as we have trustwor-

---

[5]It is debatable whether there was a historical mission during the ministry, or to what extent the Gospel description of it has been colored by the later image of the Twelve as apostles in the postresurrectional Christian missionary enterprise. That postresurrectional coloring does occur in Gospel descriptions is also affirmed by the Instruction mentioned in the preceding footnote (BRCFC 113).

[6]"Judas of James" appears in the lists of the Twelve in Luke and Acts, "Thaddaeus" in the Marcan list, and "Lebbaeus" in significant textual witnesses to the Matthean list (Matt 10:3). The facile claim that these are three names for the one man may be challenged by the invitation to supply examples of one man bearing three Semitic names, none of which is a patronymic.

thy information. One may suspect that they did not, but we have no proof.

As for exercising supervision, there is no NT evidence that any of the Twelve ever served as heads of local Churches; and it is several centuries before they begin to be described as "bishops" of first-century Christian centers, a description which is surely an anachronism.[7] According to Acts 6:2 and 15:6, the Twelve exercised a type of collective influence in meetings that decided church policy. The Twelve are regarded as having a foundational role, either collectively as their names appear on the twelve foundations of the heavenly Jerusalem (Rev 21:14), or in the person of Peter (Matt 16:18), or with Peter and John as two of the pillars (of the Church) in Gal 2:9. An important text for supervisory authority is Matt 18:18, where the disciples (probably the Twelve) are given the power to bind and loose, whether that means admitting to the community or making binding regulations. This power is given specifically to Peter in Matt 16:19; and in Acts 5:1–6 we find him striking down unworthy members of the community. Also in John 21:15–17 Peter is told by Jesus to feed or pasture Jesus' sheep.[8] Thus there is the image of a collective policy-making authority for the Twelve in the NT; and in the case of Peter, the best known of the Twelve, there is the memory of pastoral responsibility. Otherwise the NT is remarkably vague about the kind of supervision exercised by members of the Twelve.

THE HELLENIST LEADERS AND JAMES OF JERUSALEM

Acts 6:1–6 is a key scene in telling us how Luke understood supervision in the early Church. The Christians in Jerusalem are becoming numerous; and a dispute has broken out whereby one group

---

[7]In particular, D. W. O'Connor, *Peter in Rome* (New York: Columbia Univ., 1969) 207, contends that the idea that Peter served as the first bishop of Rome can be traced back no further than the third century. We have no convincing evidence that the custom of having a single bishop prevailed in Rome before the middle of the second century.

[8]One of the two Greek verbs in this passage, *poimainein,* involves guiding, feeding, and guarding. However, it should be underlined that Peter cannot call the sheep his own; they remain Jesus' sheep, as we saw in Chapter Six.

of Jewish Christians (Hebrews), who exercise control of community goods, is shutting off aid to the widows as the most vulnerable members of the other group of Jewish Christians (Hellenists).[9] The basis of the dispute was probably theological, stemming from the negative Hellenist attitude toward the Temple (to be revealed in Stephen's sermon in Acts 7:47–51). The Twelve summon the common Christian assembly called "the multitude,"[10] and they discuss the problem. According to Luke, therefore, by the mid-30s there has already developed some structure for handling the common goods and also a deliberative assembly. But now more formal administration is needed to deal with a larger and less harmonious membership.

There are three results from this scene: (1) Even to settle the dispute, the Twelve will not take over the distribution of community goods: "It is not right that we should give up preaching the word of God in order to serve tables." The fact that this is mentioned as a refused possibility means that the Twelve have not been taking care of food distribution. The decision of the Twelve to avoid becoming administrators of the local Church confirms the statement made above that none of the Twelve is portrayed as a local Church supervisor in NT times. (2) At the suggestion of Peter, the Hellenists are given their own administrators, whose (seven) names are listed in Acts 6:5. The fact that this dispute has been centered on the distribution of food, described as "waiting [*diakonein*] on table," has led to the *erroneous* designation of the Hellenist leaders as deacons, with the thought that they were the second-level church administrators mentioned in Philip 1:1 and the Pastorals. However, they seem to have been the top-level administrators for the Hellenist Christians, who not only supervised the distribution of the common goods but also preached and taught (as seen from Stephen's sermon in Acts 7

---

[9]The likelihood is that the Hellenists were Jews (by birth or conversion) who spoke only Greek (whence the name) and were heavily acculturated in the Greco-Roman society (the totally Greek names of the seven leaders). The particular group of Hellenists described in Acts 6 had come to believe in Jesus.

[10]*Plēthos* in Acts 6:2, 5 and 15:12, 30 seems to be a technical designation, related to Qumran terminology where the community meeting was called a "Session of the Many" (IQS 6:8ff.).

and Philip's activity in Acts 8).[11] They are the first local church administrators encountered in the NT. We do not know if they had a
title, but aspects of the *episkopē* exercised by presbyter-bishops later
in the first century resemble the tasks of the Hellenist leaders. (3) We
are not told in Acts 6 that the Hebrew section of the Jerusalem community received a corresponding set of administrators, but subsequent information in Acts causes us to suspect that they did. In Acts
11:30 we find a reference to a group of presbyters (*presbyteroi*) who
are in charge of the common food of the Jerusalem/Judean
Church—a Church from which the Hellenists have been driven out
by Jewish persecution.[12]

The structure of the Jerusalem Church needs special attention.
The presbyters are consistently mentioned alongside the "apostles "
(Acts 15:2, 4, 6, 22, 23; 16:4), a term which for Luke means the
Twelve. This twin set of Christian authorities has parallels to Luke's
description of a twin set of Jewish authorities: the rulers of the people
and the presbyters/elders (Acts 4:5, 8), or the high priests and the
presbyters/elders (Acts 23:14; 25:15). While this parallelism may
stem from Luke, it is not unlikely that the Jewish Christians of Jerusalem took over the idea of presbyters from the Jewish synagogue. Occasionally Luke singles out on the Jewish side a spokesman, e.g., a high
priest such as Annas or Ananias, alongside the presbyters/elders
(Acts 24:1; see 4:6); so also on the Christian side he singles out James
in a presiding role among the presbyters (Acts 21:18). Luke does not
identify this James, but surely he is the James whom Paul (Gal 1:19)
locates at Jerusalem and calls "the brother of the Lord" and an apostle.[13] His importance is clear in Gal 2:9, where he is listed ahead of

---

[11] Although the Greek text is not certain, Acts 11:19–20 implies that Hellenists,
scattered in the persecution that arose over Stephen, began the mission to the Gentiles
(*Hellēnes*).

[12] Acts 8:1 indicates the selective nature of the persecution of Christians: the apostles (and presumably the Hebrew Christians) were left untouched (since they conducted no campaign against worship in the Temple), while the Hellenist Christians were
scattered and pursued.

[13] It is not absolutely clear that the phrase "none of the other apostles except
James" calls James an apostle, but that is the easier reading. He would be an apostle in
the Pauline sense, where the term is not confined to the Twelve. In light of the clear

Peter/Cephas and John (two members of the Twelve) among the reputed pillars of the Jerusalem Church. He took a leading role in the discussions at Jerusalem ca. A.D. 49 about the admission of Gentiles as Christians without their being circumcised, and also in subsequent attempts to bind these Gentiles to Jewish food laws (Acts 15:13–21, 23–29; Gal 2:2, 12). The contention that he succeeded Peter as leader of the Jerusalem Church is based on the misconception that Peter was the local leader of the Church in Jerusalem. According to Acts, the Twelve did exercise a type of leadership in the Jerusalem Church in the early days when that Church constituted all of Christendom, and Peter was the spokesman of the Twelve. But Acts 6:2 shows Peter on behalf of the Twelve refusing administration properly understood when that became necessary because of numbers and complexity. Thus it is more correct to say that from the moment that the Jerusalem Church needed precise supervision, James along with the presbyters played that role. That James was remembered as a person who exercised supervision over a Church is confirmed by the Epistle of James. Whether or not it was written by him, such an epistle with its instruction about behavior, teaching, and prayer life was thought to be attributable to him by the person who did write it. In the mid-30s, then, it would appear that the need was recognized for local supervision of the Hebrew and Hellenist communities in Jerusalem[14] and was met in two different ways, respectively, by James and the presbyters and by the seven Hellenist authorities. Each of these supervisory groups would have managed the distribution of the common funds, made decisions affecting the life style of Christians, and entered into discussion about church policy as regards converts. The urging of the common assembly by the Twelve (Acts 6:3) which led to this development is the closest the Twelve ever come in the NT to appointing local church leaders.

✓✓!
TOO BAD-
DICKIE!

---

distinction between the Twelve and brothers of the Lord (Acts 1:13–14; I Cor 15:5, 7), he was not one of the Twelve and therefore probably not an apostle by Lucan standards.

[14]Acts 6:1–6 is treated as having a historical substratum even by scholars not overly inclined to trust Lucan historicity. The division it portrays runs against the Lucan emphasis on one-mindedness, and it agrees with what we know about anti-Temple movements among Jewish groups.

THE PAULINE APOSTLE

In Paul's view, inevitably refracted through his own situation, apostles were those who were sent out by the risen Jesus to proclaim the gospel, even at the price of suffering and persecution. Clearly from I Cor 15:5–7 "all the apostles" were a more numerous group than the Twelve, and it is likely that this notion of apostle was ancient and more widespread than the Pauline sphere. The I Cor 15 formula is generally considered, at least in part, to be pre-Pauline. The idea of the missionary apostle was so well established that it was applied to the Twelve by those who considered them apostles.[15] For instance, Matt 28:16–20 has the risen Jesus giving to the Twelve (Eleven) a mission to the whole earth (also Acts 1:8), even though historically it cannot be shown that many of the Twelve functioned outside Jerusalem.[16]

If Paul is taken as an example of the missionary apostle, his letters supply many examples of apostolic supervision: he teaches, he exhorts, he reproves, and he exercises judgment against bad members of a Church. In II Cor 13:2 he implies that, when present, the apostle can punish directly without need for consulting the community; and II Thess 3:14 orders anyone to be ostracized who refuses to obey the apostle's instructions conveyed by letter. Nevertheless, despite relatively long periods spent by Paul at Corinth and Ephesus, the apostle is not a local, residential Church leader.

Even from the earliest days of the Pauline mission, there were

---

[15]There are many different views of apostles in the NT, and it is not possible to trace a universally valid linear development. But as regards the Twelve, the following is at least plausible: the Twelve were considered as apostles; then came the expression the "Twelve Apostles" in the sense that they were the apostles par excellence because they had been called by the earthly Jesus, as well as commissioned by the risen Jesus; then "the Twelve Apostles" in an exclusive sense. The last stage dominates in Luke, for only in Acts 14:4, 14 does Luke ever call anyone else "apostle," namely, Barnabas and Paul.

[16]Whether Paul would have agreed that most of the Twelve were apostles by his missionary standards is not known (he never calls them apostles). On the one hand, he knows that they saw the risen Jesus (I Cor 15:5); on the other hand, there is no evidence that many of them went *out* to preach the gospel. In any case, he certainly recognized Peter as an apostle (Gal 2:7).

local church leaders who functioned while the apostle was alive. About A.D. 50 Paul told the Thessalonians whom he had converted a few months before (I Thess 5:12): "Respect those who labor among you and are over you [*proistamenoi*] in the Lord." Philippians (1:1) is addressed to the *episkopoi* and *diakonoi*; and if the address of this composite letter came from Paul, it is proof that the title "supervisor" was already in use by A.D. 60; and I Cor 12:28 lists "administrations" or governance (*kybernēsis*) as a charism at Corinth. But our knowledge of local supervision during Paul's lifetime is quite limited. Among the things we do *not* know are the following: Did the local leaders at the various Pauline Churches differ in terms of the authority they exercised and the roles they played? Did they all have titles and were the titles uniform? Was theirs a true office held for a set or long period of time? What precisely did they do? Were they appointed by Paul, or were they elected by the local community, or did they come forward feeling themselves to be possessors of a charism? The appearance of leaders at Thessalonica within such a short time after Paul's evangelizing makes it quite plausible that sometimes he arranged for local leadership before he left a community. The Lucan statement in Acts 14:23 that Barnabas and Paul appointed "presbyters in every Church" is probably anachronistic in the title it gives and in the universality of the practice,[17] but probably quite correct in that during his lifetime Paul sometimes appointed local church leaders in communities he evangelized. No matter what supervision such leaders exercised, they were still subject to the overarching supervision of the apostle, who could issue commands in all the Churches (I Cor 7:17) and had a daily care for all the Churches touched by his mission (II Cor 11:28). The supervision of the local church leader was modified in another way by the presence of other charisms in the community. In I Cor 12:28 the charism of administrators is men-

---

[17]One may support this conclusion from a convergence of scattered evidence: from the instructions that had to be given to Titus (1:5) in the Pastorals; from the failure to mention bishops in the Corinthian correspondence where it would have been logical to invoke their aid; from the failure to mention presbyters in any undisputed Pauline letter; from the need of Clement in *I Corinthians* 42–44 to strengthen the episcopate/presbyterate by giving it a pedigree; from the evidence of *Didache* 15 that only gradually did bishops and deacons take over the functions of prophets and teachers (mentioned in I Cor 12:28; Eph 4:11).

tioned only after many others: "first apostles, second prophets, third teachers, then workers of miracles, then healers, helpers, *administrators.*" We do not know how such figures as prophets, teachers, and administrators were interrelated in the supervision of a community.

While the authority of the apostle seems to have been the highest (under Christ) in the Churches of his mission, there is evidence that a rivalry could develop when different apostles worked in the same community. At Corinth (I Cor 1:12) there is trouble when some proclaim adherence to Paul, others to Apollos, others to Cephas. In II Cor 11:5 Paul is sarcastic about the efforts of "superapostles " in a Church he founded. Such danger of conflicting authority causes him to avoid building upon another man's foundation (Rom 15:20), although others build upon his foundation (I Cor 3:10). It becomes important, then, that the various apostles preach the same gospel: "Whether then it was I or they, so we preached and so you believed" (I Cor 15:11). Differences of view are especially serious when they occur between an apostle like Paul and a member of the Twelve like Peter, or between either of them and the head of the Jerusalem Church, James the brother of the Lord. Although Paul is critical of the status of such "pillars"—"What they were makes no difference to me" (Gal 2:6, 9)—he recognizes that in one way or another they have enough power to render his efforts vain.[18] And so it is important that these figures extend the right hand of fellowship to Paul (Gal 2:7–9). All of this means that in facing a major problem, like that of converting the Gentiles without requiring circumcision, figures with a different type of supervision (Paul, James, Peter) all had a say in the outcome. Moreover, despite agreement on the main issue, they might well continue to disagree on other issues, e.g., on the obligation of the Gentiles to keep the Jewish food laws. Peter, who had been under the influence of Paul, changed his stance when men from James challenged his behavior at Antioch (Gal 2:12), seemingly because Antioch was within James' sphere of influence as regards such matters of Christian interrelations. According to Acts

---

[18]The text in Gal 2:2 certainly does not mean that his gospel would have to be acknowledged as wrong if they disagreed with him, for Gal 1:8 excludes that possibility. Rather, refusal by Peter, James, and John to accept the Gentiles without circumcision would have ruined Paul's efforts to keep the Gentile Churches in communion with the Jewish Churches.

15:20, 23 the policy of binding the Gentiles by Jewish food laws was advocated by James and put into force for Antioch, Syria, and Cilicia. But Paul did not insist on such a policy in the Churches of his mission (I Cor 8). However, if Acts 21:23 is historical, even though Paul may have felt free to have one policy in Corinth while James had another in Jerusalem and Antioch, when Paul came to Jerusalem he may have had to follow James' policy on Jewish obligations. Thus, when we speak of supervision exercised by the three best-known figures of the ancient Church, we have to recognize that the NT itself shows different areas of competence (both geographical and topical) for Peter, the first-listed and spokesman of the Twelve, for James, the brother of the Lord and leader of the Jerusalem (mother) Church, and for Paul, the apostle to the Gentiles.

THE PRESBYTER-BISHOPS AND THE SUCCESSION TO THE APOSTLES

If many of the Pauline Churches had local leaders during the apostle's lifetime (some of whom at least had been appointed by him), the question of local-church leadership became a major concern in the last third of the century, after the death of the great apostles in the 60s.[19] We see this in the Pastoral Epistles,[20] where Titus (1:5) has been left in Crete "to set in order what was wanting and to appoint presbyters in each city." To facilitate such appointments, the qualifications of an *episkopos*, "supervisor, bishop," are listed (Titus 1:7–11; I Tim 3:1–7). The very fact that Titus has to be told to do this means that there were not yet presbyter-bishops in all the Churches of the Pauline mission and confirms the suspicion that

---

[19] The only apostles about whom we have much biographical information in the NT are the three mentioned at the end of the preceding paragraph (Peter, James, and Paul), all of whom died in the mid-60s.

[20] Between 80% and 90% of scholarship today would regard the Pastorals as Deutero-Pauline, written after Paul's death. However, there is little agreement as to whether they belong in the late-first or early-second century. Personally, I see little reason for dating them later than the 80s and find it very difficult to believe that the situation they describe is not several decades earlier than that addressed by Ignatius of Antioch (ca. 110). The author may be saying to his times what he thinks Paul would have said were Paul alive.

Luke was anachronistic when he said that in the late 40s Barnabas and Paul appointed presbyters in *every* Church (Acts 14:23). Luke was probably describing what was going on in the Churches at the very time that he was writing Acts (80s).

We may begin our treatment of this period by noting that the Pastorals are meant to give authority to Timothy and Titus, companions of Paul, to structure Churches, even as the apostle is disappearing from the ecclesiastical scene (II Tim 4:6). There was, then, a period of postapostolic supervision by second-generation apostolic delegates who acted in the name of the apostle on the grounds that they had accompanied him and knew his mind.[21] There must have been resistance to such apostolic delegates. (If the Pastorals are pseudonymous, Paul is being summoned from the grave to still the resistance.) In I Tim 4:12 Paul is pictured as encouraging Timothy not to let himself be despised and, in II Tim 1:6, to rekindle the gift of God that is within him through the laying on of Paul's hands. Such apostolic delegates would have constituted an intermediary stage between that of the apostle's great personal authority over the Churches founded by him (40s–60s) and the period when the local Church leaders became the highest authorities (second century). We know by name only a few of these second-generation apostolic delegates who exercised quasi-apostolic authority. Were there also third-generation apostolic delegates, i.e., disciples of the disciples of the apostles, who were not local bishops? Eventually (and certainly by the second century) there disappears the apostolic function of not being closely attached to a local Church while supervising a whole group of Churches with a common heritage. It was only in a partial way, then, that the local bishops succeeded to the apostolic care for the Churches. (Later, with the development of the patriarchates and of the papacy, care for a larger group of Churches found again a vehicle of expression.) In the NT one should note that succession in pastoral care is to the apostles in the Pauline sense. The idea that the Twelve were apostles (and eventually that they were the only apos-

---

[21]There is no indication that we are to think of Titus and Timothy as presbyter-bishops; theirs is a semiapostolic role. The use of II Tim 1:6 ("Rekindle the gift of God that is within you through the laying on of my hands") as evidence for the apostolic (Pauline) ordination of bishops is very questionable.

tles to be reckoned with) would ultimately lead to the understanding that they were the apostles to whom the local church leaders succeeded. In the NT, however, the Twelve are never described as being the first to bring Christianity to an area and in that sense to establish a local Church; and so the NT never raises the issue of succession to their pastoral care.[22]

Moving on from the apostolic delegates to the local church leaders described in the Pastorals, we find that in these letters there have emerged established offices for which qualifications are given (I Tim 3; Titus 1). Some of the qualifications are institutional, so that no matter what abilities a person may have, that person can be rejected because of stipulations that are only secondarily related to what the person will be doing, e.g., no recent convert nor a person who has been married a second time is eligible to be a presbyter. This factor, plus the idea of appointment of presbyter-bishops by an apostolic delegate, means that personally experienced or claimed charisms have ceded to community acknowledgment in determining who shall have supervision. Unfortunately, outside of these three letters which deal with apostolic delegates, we know very little about how communities at this period did determine who would have supervision. *Didache* 15:1 indicates that the community itself could select leaders; but in other areas and times it may well have been that the leaders of sister-churches intervened, or that the presbyter-bishops sought to have their own children succeed them. There is nothing in the NT literature about a regular process of ordination. (And *a fortiori* there is nothing to support the thesis that, by a chain of laying on of hands, *every* local presbyter-bishop could trace a pedigree of ordination back to "the apostles."[23]) Nor do we know whether church offices were held for a limited time or for life.

Let us now turn to the designation of local church officials.[24] In

---

[22]See, however, the discussion of I Peter below, n. 31.

[23]For ecumenical purposes, a study should be made on how the impression has been created (erroneously in my judgment) that such a "tactile" succession is a doctrine of the Roman Catholic Church.

[24]It is not germane to this paper on church supervision to discuss other community roles or orders recognized in the Pastorals (and other NT works), e.g., widows and virgins, since they are not recorded as having exercised "supervision."

the Pastorals there are two offices set up for the pastoral care of the community, a higher office and a subordinate office. If we invoke wider NT evidence, it seems that the holder of each of these offices had two designations, respectively, the presbyter (elder) or bishop, and the "younger" or deacon. One document may speak exclusively of *episkopoi*, "bishops," and *diakonoi*, "deacons" (Philip 1:1), while another document may speak of *presbyteroi*, "elders," and *neōteroi*, "youngers" (I Pet 5:1, 5). Still other passages illustrate the interchangeability of the respective titles. The interchangeability of *presbyteros* and *episkopos* is seen not only in the Pastorals (Titus 1:5–7; I Tim 3:1; 5:17) but also in Acts 20:28, where those who have previously been designated as the *presbyteroi* of Ephesus are told, "Take heed to yourselves and to all the flock in which the Holy Spirit has made you *episkopoi* to shepherd the Church of God." Similarly, in I Pet 5:2–3 Peter addresses himself to the *presbyteroi*, "Feed the flock, being supervisors (*episkopountes*) not by coercion but willingly."[25] The interchangeability of *neōteros* and *diakonos* is attested by the parallelism in Luke 22:16: "Let the great one among you become as a *neōteros*; let the one who rules become as a *diakonos*." The fact that *neōteros*, "younger," is not simply an age bracket (any more than is *presbyteros*, "elder") but another name for the subordinate office[26] has frequently been missed, resulting in strange combinations, e.g., while the reference in I Pet 5:1–4 to *presbyteroi* has rightly been understood as a designation not simply for elderly men but for the holders of presbyteral office, the next verse (5:5) is (wrongly) thought to shift with its *neōteroi* to the theme of youth!

If we concentrate on the higher office, it has often been suggested that one title, *presbyteros*, was in use among Jewish Christian communities, while the other, *episkopos*, was in use in the Gentile Churches. However, the evidence that we have for the use of *presbyteros* among Jewish Christians comes from Acts' account of the Jerusalem community (see section above on Hellenist Leaders and James

---

[25] The *episkopountes* is textually dubious, since it is missing from Codex Vaticanus and from the original hand of Sinaiticus.

[26] A seminal treatment of this subject is that of J. H. Elliott, "Ministry and Church Order in the NT: A Traditio-Historical Analysis (I Pt 5, 1–5 and plls.)," *CBQ* 32 (1970) 367–91.

of Jerusalem), and the same book describes the officials of the Gentile Christian communities as *presbyteroi* too (Acts 14:23; 20:17). A more plausible theory is that we have here a reflection of two strains of Judaism which came into Christianity. The synagogues of Pharisaic Judaism had a group of *zĕqēnîm,* "elders," the Hebrew equivalent of *presbyteroi,* forming a council whose members set policy but were not pastors responsible for the spiritual care of individuals. In addition to such *zĕqēnîm,* the Dead Sea Scrolls community of the New Covenant had officials who bore the title *mĕbaqqēr* or *pāqîd,* synonymous words meaning "supervisor, overseer," the Hebrew equivalent of *episkopos.* These functionaries, assigned one to a group, did have a pastoral responsibility. The higher of the two Christian offices described in the Pastorals may have combined the group of presbyters from the Pharisaic synagogue with the supervisor of Jewish sectarianism, so that the presbyters served also in a supervisory capacity. This origin would explain why in Titus 1:5 *presbyteroi* are spoken of in the plural, while in 1:7, obviously referring to the same office, the author describes the *episkopos* in the singular. Furthermore, while our NT evidence points to a general interchangeability between the titles *presbyteros* and *episkopos,* it is possible that not all the presbyters of a community assumed the title and role of the supervisor. In I Tim 5:17 we are told that a double honor is due to "those presbyters who rule well."[27] Does the author mean that, while all the presbyters rule, only some rule well, or that only some presbyters rule? The latter seems more plausible, since he goes on in the same verse to single out those presbyters "who labor in preaching and teaching," which surely means that not all had those tasks. The body of presbyters, then, may have divided up among themselves tasks once handled by people with different charisms, e.g., by the teachers and administrators of I Cor 12:28. It is well known that Ignatius of Antioch gives witness to the (recent) emergence of a three-fold-office structure in certain communities: one *episkopos,* under him a group of *presbyteroi* and a group of *diakonoi* (a structure nowhere clearly attested in the NT), so that the title *episkopos* is now no longer widely interchangeable with *presbyteros.* However, in light

---

[27]"Rule" is the participial form *proestōtes,* from *proistēmi,* the verb used for church leaders in I Thess 5:12.

of the discussion above, attention should be paid to Polycarp, *Philippians* 5:3, for there *neōteroi* are told to be subject to both presbyters and deacons. Just as ultimately presbyters became subject to bishops, so *neōteroi* became subordinate to *diakonoi*; and it seems that at least for a brief period the two sets of terms yielded four offices or roles.

That the term *diakonos* could be applied to a woman is known from Rom 16:1.[28] In the passage on deacons in I Tim 3:8–13, rules are laid down for women in 3:11, and some have argued that these are the wives of the deacons. (However, the clear reference to the deacon's wife in 3:12 may be introducing a new but related topic.) Whether they are or not, they surely serve as deacons, since the author speaks of the rules for them as similar to the rules for (male) deacons. In view of the high plausibility that there were men and women deacons in the Churches of the Pastorals, and that *neōteros* was another term for *diakonos*, a passage in I Tim 5:1–2 raises the question of whether there were also both men and women presbyters.[29] The apostolic delegate is told by "Paul" how to treat presbyters and "youngers": "Do not rebuke a *presbyteros* but exhort him as you would a father, and the *neōteroi* as you would brothers; *presbyterai* as you would mothers, and *neōterai* as you would sisters." It is most often assumed that age brackets are meant, and indeed *neōterai* refers to younger women who are widows in 5:11, 14. Nevertheless, every other passage dealing with *presbyteros* in the Pastorals is taken to refer to officeholders, including two passages in this same chapter of I Timothy (5:17, 19). This argument is offset by the fact that the parallel passage in Titus 2:1–6 (which speaks of the male *presbytēs* and *neōteros* and the female *presbytis* and *nea*) deals with age groups. In any case, we can say that *if* there were women presbyters as there were women deacons, it should be remembered that not all presbyters seem to have ruled (i.e., served as an *episkopos*). The prohibition in I Tim 2:12, "I do not permit a woman to teach or or to have au-

---

[28] In my judgment, it is better to speak of female deacons than of deaconesses, a term which can be confused with a later church institution that did not have the ordained status of the deacon.

[29] Aquila and Prisca offer the example of a man and a woman in roles that might be considered presbyteral, e.g., they have a house church in their home (I Cor 16:19) and they "took" Apollos and instructed him in the way of God (Acts 18:26)

thority over men," may have been thought all the more necessary if women held an office that allowed many of its male occupants to teach and rule.

What were the precise supervisory roles of the presbyter-bishops and the *neōteroi*-deacons? Only the qualifications, not the activities, of the deacons are given in I Tim 3:8–13; and so we know nothing about what they did.[30] Since the name *diakonos* describes a servant, perhaps the deacon in NT times really did not exercise much supervision. As for the presbyter-bishops, we know that some or many taught (I Tim 5:17). In particular, they are associated with refuting false doctrine and protecting the purity of community faith (Titus 1:9). From the insistence that the presbyter-bishop must be able to manage his own household, being no lover of money (I Tim 3:3–5; also I Pet 5:2, "not for shameful gain"), and from the rhetorical question, "If someone does not know how to manage his own household, how can he care for the Church of God?" (I Tim 3:5), we may suspect that presbyters had responsibilities toward the common goods of the community. The image of the shepherd appears frequently for the presbyter-bishop (Acts 20:28; I Pet 5:2), and so his supervising authority was like that of a shepherd over sheep, feeding, guiding, and protecting. It is scarcely accidental that in the Dead Sea Scrolls community of the New Covenant similar roles were assigned to the "supervisor" (CD 13:7–19): he is like a shepherd over sheep; he manages the common goods; he is a teacher and inspector of the doctrine of the members of the community.

No cultic or liturgical role is assigned to the presbyter-bishops in the Pastorals. The closest to that in the NT is James 5:14–15, where the presbyters of the Church are called in to pray over the sick person and anoint him in the name of the Lord, so that "the prayer of faith will save the sick person." This passage in James confirms the existence of presbyters in a non-Pauline Church of Jewish origins where the name of James (the brother of the Lord) was venerated, and may be related to the information found in Acts about James *and the presbyters* at Jerusalem. Another work, I Pet 5:1–4, ad-

---

[30]That the deacons waited upon table is an idea stemming from the false assumption that deacons were involved in Acts 6:1–6. The deacon Phoebe is an apostolic "helper" (Rom 16:2: *prostatis*—see n. 27 above) to Paul and others.

dressed to Gentile Churches of northern Asia Minor, shows the existence of presbyter-bishops in an area where evidently Peter was looked upon as an authority.[31] The idea that Peter spoke as a "fellow presbyter" telling presbyters how to behave is not unlike that of Paul in the Pastorals giving the qualifications for presbyter-bishops. Thus, in Churches associated with the three great apostolic figures of the NT, Paul, James, and Peter, presbyters were known and established in the last third of the century.

In the letters of Ignatius of Antioch the bishop has unique authority in relation to baptism and the eucharist, but we find no word of this in the NT. In comparison with the silence as regards presbyter-bishops, various figures are said to baptize, e.g., members of the Twelve (Matt 28:19; Acts 2:41; 10:48), Philip the Hellenist leader (Acts 8:38), and Paul the apostle (I Cor 1:14–17—but "Christ did not send me to baptize"). As for the eucharist, we know virtually nothing of who presided in NT times. The instruction "Do this" in commemoration of Jesus is given to the Twelve in Luke 22:19 (I Cor 11:24), but not in Mark/Matthew. According to Acts 13:2, in the Church of Antioch prophets and teachers "liturgize" (*leitourgein*). This finds an echo in *Didache* 10:7, "Allow the prophets to 'eucharistize' [*eucharistein*] as they will."[32] Between the NT position, where prophets and teachers have a liturgical role, and the Ignatian position, where bishops and presbyters have that role, comes (logically and perhaps chronologically) the situation in *Didache*.[33] In the Church addressed by that work there are still prophets and teachers, with prophets conducting the eucharist; yet the author urges, "Appoint for yourselves bishops and deacons . . . for they are your honorable men together with prophets and teachers" (*Didache* 15:1–2).

We have spoken about Churches that did have presbyter-bishops toward the end of the first century; for other NT churches of

---

[31]Letters of pastoral concern, closely similar to Pauline style, attributed to Peter, portray him as having an apostolic care for specific Churches and confirm the observation that of the Twelve Peter came closest to the Pauline notion of an apostle.

[32]Association of the prophet with the eucharist is not so strange when we realize that the NT prophets, men and women, often know and predict the future; and the eucharist was thought to proclaim "the Lord's death *until he comes*" (I Cor 11:26).

[33]A chronology that has considerable plausibility in my mind is ca. 80–90 for the Pastorals, ca. 100 for the *Didache,* and 110 for the Ignatian letters.

that period, we do not know how supervision was structured. Matthew has clear ideas on how authority is properly exercised (18:15–18) but tells us nothing about the officials in the Church who might be doing this. He knows of Christian prophets (10:41) and of Christian scribes (13:52); and so some have surmised that Matthew's was a community with prophets and scribes, but not yet presbyter-bishops and *neōteroi*-deacons. This would be a stage of structure less developed as regards office than that attested in *Didache*, a work that has Matthean affinities. In any case, Matthew will not let those who teach be called rabbi, for there is only one teacher, Christ. Nor will he let community members be called leaders (pl. of *kathēgētēs*), for Christ is the only leader. Nor is anyone to be called father (Matt 23:8–10). In this he differs from some other NT texts where there are human teachers (I Cor 12:28–29; Eph 4:11; I Tim 2:7) and an apostle who describes himself as a father toward his community (I Cor 4:15). The fascination with developing structure and offices in the late first century had its dangers, and Matthew was alert to these.

SUPERVISION IN THE JOHANNINE COMMUNITY

Also alert to the danger of human authorities were the Johannine writers.[34] John 21, which most think of as a late Johannine addition to the Gospel, ascribes the role of shepherd to Peter but *not* to the Beloved Disciple. This probably means that the role of the human shepherd had not been part of the community's religious tradition and was only now coming in from the outside (whence the need to assure the readers that Jesus authorized it). For an earlier stage in the community history, the image of Jesus as the shepherd (John 10) was sufficient.

The author of II–III John (who probably wrote I John as well) calls himself "the presbyter"; but in the three Epistles he does not

---

[34]Increasingly the view that two different writers were responsible for the Gospel and the Epistles is gaining ground. A very high percentage of critical scholars thinks that no Johannine work was written by one of the Twelve or by the Beloved Disciple. The identity of the latter remains a mystery, although it is plausible that he was a companion of Jesus, an influential force in the community's history, and a source for the Evangelist.